GR Dale
Jun '05

A Measure of Munros

Graham Wilson

A MEASURE OF MUNROS

illustrated by Gerry Dale

Millrace

First published in Great Britain in 2005 by
Millrace
2a Leafield Road, Disley
Cheshire SK12 2JF
www.millracebooks.co.uk

Text © 2005 Graham Wilson
Illustrations © 2005 Gerry Dale

ISBN: 1 902173 18X

Typeset in Berthold Baskerville.
Printed and bound in the United Kingdom
by Cromwell Press Ltd, Trowbridge, Wiltshire.

Acknowledgements

Anyone who chooses to write about mountaineering in Scotland must, explicitly or implicitly, pay tribute to the contribution of the Scottish Mountaineering Club and the various editors of and contributors to its Journal and guides. I would, therefore, like to thank the Club for permission to quote from a variety of articles. I would recommend *A Century of Scottish Mountaineering*, a selected anthology of such writing, as an ideal introduction to what is a remarkable archive. Scottish mountaineering has never been short of writers with talent, and there is no doubt that I owe much to such exponents, ranging from Bill Murray to Tom Patey, who aroused and sustained my interest in mountains and mountain literature at large. Finally, many thanks to family and friends who enabled me, one way or another, to complete not only the Munros but also the following account.

GPW

Contents

An introduction of sorts

The car, as usual, wended its way through the leafy Cheshire lanes. The weather, as usual, was warm and bright. For it seemed that the annual general meeting for which we were bound deliberately chose, on an annual basis, one of the finer days of the year to keep us indoors. Inevitably the driver would, at one point, observe, *What a waste*, and I would agree. The waste was of the weather and how it could be put to better use, climbing or walking. Talk would then turn to enquiries about holiday plans, which on this occasion must have included Scotland.

Done many of the Scottish hills?

Not really. Saving them for my middle age. Perhaps my tone was a touch too lofty, for there was a slight pause.

Better get cracking then.

And that, I suppose, is how it started. That is to say, mountain climbing in Scotland on a regular basis, rather than Munro-bagging. Of course, I had no intention of following the latter nugatory course of action. I knew little about the activity, other than that it was generally frowned upon by the writers I particularly admired. The scornful words of D J Frazer's pastiche of Browning's 'Lost Leader'

> *Just for a handful of summits he left us,*
> *Just for a 'Dearg' to tick on his list.*

rang in my ears and its implication was firmly stuck in my mind. If Scottish hills were to be visited, they would have substance of their own and not depend for their reputation on some altimetric coincidence. So, stung into action by the perceived slight on my physical prowess, I immediately organised visits to the Cairngorms and Torridon on the grounds they were two places I had *(a)* heard of and *(b)* could safely locate on a map.

Not that the rest of Scotland was entirely unknown territory. An early family holiday in Galloway had included a trip around the surrounding hills. I can't remember much about them, other than that my brother complained (as it turned out, with some justification) of feeling unwell and a rapid descent to the valley where my father commandeered a passing car and one-third requested, two-thirds demanded that his younger son be transported to the appropriate hotel in Dumfries. Later, there was the odd boating/climbing holiday on the west coast, where we spent most of the time dodging the ghillies and in the process, no doubt, disturbing the deer. And then there was Skye.

Although my first visit was close to fifty years ago, details still stand out. The continuous narrative has gone but the substantives remain firmly printed. Leaving Newcastle in a sleeper for Fort William, being shunted around the Glasgow sidings in the middle of the night, a wondrous journey to Mallaig in a train with an observation car, playing darts in a pub adorned with a stuffed gannet in full flight. Bus journeys to Broadford and Sligachan and the first sight of the Cuillin and the last pint for a fortnight before we were trucked off to the Youth Hostel in temperate Glen Brittle. The first day was perfect. An early start into Coire Lagan. Two and a half thousand feet up and down the cliff of Sron na Ciche, carefully working through the grades, sorting out the lie of the land and the adhesive properties of gabbro.

When all this was to our satisfaction, we continued along the ridge to Sgurr Alasdair which, as a first

Munro, is probably as good as it gets. We must also have passed over the Tops of Sgurr Sgumain and Sgurr Thearlaich, without really realising their significance. We completed the round of Coire Lagan, though whether we traversed Sgurr Mhic Coinnich by Collie's Ledge or climbed it by King's Chimney is now long forgotten. One thing is certain, we must have passed the Inaccessible Pinnacle but I can't recall noticing it and I certainly didn't realise its significance to would-be Munroists. After all, a 125ft Moderate was scarcely likely to attract the attention of a party which was already planning next day to climb the classic combination of the Cioch Direct and the Crack of Doom – a route we had followed, so to speak, many a time on the pages of Bill Murray's account, which deemed it the 'best climb in the Cuillin' and, in his day, the 'hardest'. We sat by the cairn of Sgurr Dearg watching the sunset form before scrambling down for supper. Would the Cuillin offer enough to satisfy our ambitions? *Red skye at night...* (Experienced visitors to the island should complete the couplet according to taste.)

For the next thirteen days it rained. Not all the time. At its worst, it restricted us to the breezeblock overspill of the Youth Hostel that was our temporary lot. When the rain relented to the vertical, we ventured out to endure the dubious delights of a cascade of water running down an anorak arm as you reached for a hold (no such niceties as elasticated cuffs) or plodging ankle-deep through the inland seas that had formed at the foot of each pitch of the easy descent routes. Despite our original plans, we chose not to investigate the particular properties that distinguished the Very Severe Waterpipe Gully from its fellow conduits. When matters got really desperate, although outwith the budget, we tramped the sixteen miles to and from the Sligachan Hotel to cheer momentarily the inner man. Most days were a triumph of hope over experience, but the rock, apart from the odd slice of basalt, was easier to stick on than slide off. Eventually we outbored the weather and, in the palest of sunshine which would have disgraced the feeblest winter's day, Murray's *tour de force* was at last accomplished. This was the first of many visits and, unwittingly, the remaining Munros were ticked off, as the ridge was explored and finally completed.

An early step to being involved in the more witting collection of selected lumps of rock and peat adorned with bits of low-lying flora occurred on a second and snowclad visit to Torridon. As I was with a large party that I had somehow latched on to, I was not privy to the exact nature of a rather heated discussion that at one stage broke out. It seemed to be of an arithmetical nature and centred around the metric height of 914 and its equivalence, or otherwise, to 3,000 feet and, more especially, whether some minor protuberance to our left should be included in the expedition. Eventually the senior wrangler got his way and we trooped off to the other end of the plateau, 'just to be on the safe side'. A fellow traveller confided that this particular wart of Ossa might be, or even, as a result of future official investigation, could be, a Top. Even though the word was spoken, the upper case shone through and in a moment of innocence I asked what he meant by the term for, surely, the top had to be the top?

Never was heathen savage in deepest Africa subjected to the missionary zeal that fell about my ears. There followed a potted history of the perpetrator of the sacred Tables, Sir Hugh T Munro, Bart of Lindertis, the doings of the Scottish Mountaineering Club, and the first completionist, the Revd A E Robertson, who, legend has it, surprisingly kissed the final cairn and his wife in that order – the surprise being, I

Sir Hugh Munro

supposed, that she was there at all, rather than in the kitchen supervising the polishing of his second-best boots. Nor was the list compiled by Munro set in stone. A Variorum Table produced by Robin Campbell in 1999 shows that the five versions to date had produced between them 591 Tops, yet only 413 have had the same status in any one version. Thus, 178 mountains have come and gone, been wooed and spurned, in little over a hundred years. Such seemed the possibility for confusion that I surmised that, like the weather, there must be some sort of telephonic Munrowatch that could be contacted before setting out on the hill.

My return journey was via Fort William and, whilst browsing through the bookshelves of a well-known climbing shop, I came across a copy of the first metric edition of a revised edition of the new edition of 1953, which at the time was the ultimate word on the subject of Sir Hugh's bills of fare. So, just out of curiosity, you understand, and in case it (they) might prove useful, I bought a copy. One thing led to another and, to pass the journey, I decided to calculate how many I had actually done. Skye was encouraging. Apart from that, a clutch in the Cairngorm, a sprinkling in the north west and a family expedition to the top of Ben Nevis was the best I could muster. I had visited other mountains on more than one occasion – Buachaille Etive Mor and Bidean nam Bian to name but two – but I had never got round to going to the top. Perhaps there is some riposte to Frazer's condemnation of the unassuming footsoldier that equally execrates the climber, the limit of whose ambition is the lump of rock immediately in front of his nose.

I then began to co-ordinate the sketch maps in the book with the ground the train was passing through and by the time we reached Loch Long I realised that I must have been almost within touching distance of some forty or fifty hills which were graced by the title, Munro. There was, however, one affair that puzzled me. Despite my failings in Glencoe, I knew that I had been to the top of Garbh Bheinn, the highest point in the district of Ardgour. For, once more, we had followed not only in Murray's footsteps in our ascent of the Great Gully, but also his advice to visit the summit of a hill that enjoyed 'one of the great panoramas of Scotland'. Yet, no matter how I searched, I could find no mention of Garbh Bheinn in the Munro Tables. At last the truth was revealed. An inferior table showed to my disappointment that it was only 2,835 feet above sea level and as such didn't count. How quickly does the rot set in.

No sooner had I purchased my copy of the Tables than, inevitably, a new and revised version appeared. I dithered about further investment but it turned out money well spent. Suddenly, without stepping a foot outdoors, I found that I had conquered further and greater heights and, mercifully, an insignificant lump that I had omitted in Glen Feshie had been stripped of its Mountain laurels and cashiered to the rank of Top. It was therefore only a matter of time before I was sitting in a bar in Tobermory, writing postcards which announced the completion of my final Munro and thanking the recipients for their friendship and support during the venture.

However, mature consideration made me consider what it was that I had actually completed. Yes, I had been to the top of the 277 designated hills that were currently on offer, but were they Munros, or rather Munro's, and what would the implication be if someone decided they weren't either, or both? As

Campbell's history of change has shown, there has been a considerable movement. Opening a page of his Variorum at random, I have only to glance through a dozen entries to find Beinn Teallach making its first appearance in the fifth version and Carn Ballach making its last in the first. It may well be that the originator did not intend his summits to be wrenched out of their context in the way they have. After all, he only produced two tables: *(1) Tops Arranged According to Districts* and *(2) Tops Arranged in Order of Altitude.* There is no separate Munro Table of Mountains. And, even if he had meant such a thing, I am sure he would have been bemused that the mildly eccentric hobby of a Victorian gentleman should have caused such an explosion of commercial activity, rearrangement of deer forests and questions in the House.

One
The reason why

The Revd A E Robertson, the first person to ascend all the separate mountains contained in Munro's Tables, recalled a conversation where he was discussing with an acquaintance the merits of climbing to the top of such summits in Scotland. His listener seems not to have shared the first completionist's enthusiasm, suggesting that you might as well kiss all the lamp-posts in Princes Street. The implication being that, as no one would kiss – or at least admit to kissing – all the illuminations in Edinburgh's principal shopping thoroughfare, the ascent of all Scotland's mountains was equally ludicrous. Whilst I have to admit that there has been the odd occasion, on struggling up a peat-bump through freshly fallen snow, when the thought of embracing lamp-posts, with suitable excursions to the local hostelry, seemed relatively attractive, I tend to side with Robertson in his dismissal of the analogy. Nevertheless, the argument for the prosecution does pose the larger question of why anyone should decide to collect anything at all and, after that matter is resolved, why Munros.

As most people see order and form in terms of their own life cycle, that is, a process having a beginning and end with a steady progression between, the collection of a finite number of anything seems instinctively a sensible thing to do. Philosophers may argue otherwise, asserting that life is not a question of staggering from one pool of light to the next cast by the gig-lamps of Princes (or, for that matter, any other) Street, but rather an all-embracing amalgam of past, present and future. On the other hand, Munroists, when going the extra mile of two-up-one-down scree to avoid leaving an isolated summit in the middle of nowhere, tend to have, at that particular moment in the time–space continuum, their own views on whether matter or matters should come to a definite end. Though it has to be admitted, such is the human condition, that once back at base, even they, with the encouraging benefits of liquid warmth, take a more eclectic view of the nature of things.

As an example of this armchair optimism, I once had a design to do at least one climb on all the cliffs, crags and various protuberances listed in E C Pyatt's book *Where to Climb in the British Isles*. The sights were quickly lowered to all the cliffs, crags, etc, in the north of England, then to those where the names appeared in upper case to indicate particular worth. Finally, I settled for those which I, in my better judgment, regarded as worthwhile. As this latter list corresponded exactly with the cliffs I had in fact visited, I was able to retire gracefully, mission accomplished. Such is the usual outcome of boundless ambition. But those who collect Munros can, perhaps uniquely, have it both ways. Like the dates of the more mystical celebrations of the Christian faith, the mountains and tops are movable feasts and, as has been recorded, can therefore vary in number and nature. Yet, at any particular point in time, the number and nature is fixed. So it is quite possible to be in the interesting metaphysical state of having both completed and, at one and the same time, not completed the task. This is particularly advantageous to those who publicly despise the baggers, whilst privately ticking off their own collection.

But the affair may have more hidden depths. The gerunds 'bagging' and 'bashing' are often suffixed to the main noun in question. As the former is usually related to the collection of defenceless birds and animals through the use of explosives, there does appear to be an unfortunate air of triumphalism attached to the activity. 'Bashing' is even more pejorative, being defined by the OED as 'giving a hard time to' various parts of the anatomy or to groups of workers trying to preserve their minimal rights. As the number of aspirants increases, so the poor hills will get even more bashed and if we don't heed Othello's explanation as to why we harm the objects of our affection, then the Highlands could end up like the Pennine Way. However, at the moment, commercial activities organised by restaurateurs and not-particularly-big game hunters have a head start on Munroists on bulldozing the hills into oblivion.

I suspect that these pejorative terms are mostly used by those who look down their noses at the mere pedestrian hillgoer. In fact, the distinction between the climber and the walker seems to have existed from the very beginnings of mountaineering in Scotland. In the second volume of the SMC's Journal, the Loretto headmaster, Hely Almond, explains the division. The first group (the Ultramontane) consists of those who 'look upon a quarry face with fond enthusiasm, as affording chances quite as great, and nearly as glorious, of getting badly hurt, as a genuine mountain does'. The second (the Salvationists), as the name implies, concentrate first and foremost on making sure that they are 'absolutely safe' and are the sort of people who 'would rather go home to dinner than lie on the ground till people came to set our bones or carry us off on a stretcher'. Almond confirms that he is firmly enlisted in the Salvation Army and suspects that more members of the Club than care to admit it are also. Perhaps that puts the finger on the popularity of the game: the hills are potentially glorious, yet the ways of the Munroist are safe.

Old Glencoe Road

But perhaps the most attractive proposition to the hillwalker is the nature of the task. Two hundred and eighty four separate hills, given a concerted campaign, is a reasonable but not easy achievement. It lies in the no man's land between what can be confidently accomplished and what is probably out of the question. All the more so if your base is somewhere near the Great Glen, which would allow regular weekend access. The Sassenach is not so fortunate and must rely on holidays or, if lucky, suitable business trips. If you assume that you can average somewhere between two and three peaks per outing, then the commitment will be between fourteen and twenty weeks of Highland walking. Our man in Fort William, if he were to spend a day a week on his chosen recreational activity, could complete the round in a couple of years and still have time to appease the family with holidays on the Costas. Whereas Mick or Michaela from Manchester and points south may well have to devote a decade or two to the task, whilst demonstrating considerable skill in the delicate negotiations with the various domestic departments of War and Finance.

Once the decision has been taken, you quickly realise that there is more to it than pleasurable exercise. What you have in front of you is the opportunity to discover a whole country. For, though a subdivision of another political subdivision, the Highlands have a culture and physical uniqueness that merits such a separate description. My first reaction was one of bewilderment. I really had no sense of where I was going. The hills I knew at that time, I knew quite well. If you had asked me to plan a high-level route from Skiddaw to the top of Coniston Old Man, or a road-avoiding valley-crossing from Ennerdale to Haweswater, I would have been able, without recourse to the map, to trace in my mind's eye the ground over which the journeys would pass. In other words, I knew the area sufficiently well that I could historically connect the memories from one day's outing with those of another.

This was not true of the Munros. If you travel to your starting point of the day's walk by road, each group of mountains seems to exist as a separate entity, a bubble dissociated from the hills around it. A day in Glen Lyon seems very remote from a day on the hills above the Bridge of Orchy but, in reality, they are next-door neighbours. Stuchd an Lochain, at the west end of Glen Lyon, is only half a dozen miles away from the slopes of Beinn a' Chreachain which seem to soar above the rail traveller on the crossing of Rannoch Moor but, as they appear on different Ordnance Survey maps and the lines of approach to the day's starting point are equally separate, it is much harder to place them in perspective than a similar grouping in the Lake District. In the same way, those two gems of the north-west seaboard, Ben Sgritheall and Ladhar Bheinn, are only an eagle's wingflip or three from summit to summit across Loch Hourn. Yet the tourist would have to drive seventy, then walk five or six miles, to even paw at the foothills and would be unlikely to include both in a day's outing.

Nor, for my part, was it just the geography. I knew little or nothing of the social and political history of the area – that, for example, to refer to Buachaille Etive Mor as the 'Big Shepherd of Etive', as has been done in a number of guides to the area, was a *faux pas* of some considerable order. The correct translation is 'Herdsman', as sheep were only introduced when the human beings were cleared off by landowning commercial interests. Making an attempt to understand the language is more than a social nicety. To comprehend how the name of a hill often contains clues as to appearance and underfoot-going can be of more than academic interest if matters have gone awry in the mist or you have managed to misplace your compass.

Perhaps another hidden motive is the desire to see your name in print. The volume that contains the Munro Tables also lists the names of all those who have completed the round. In my original edition of 1974 there were 107 such names but, such is the exponential nature of the game, it is now around 4,000. Any attempt to pin down the exact number is fraught with problems. Even if you had the equivalent to the Archangel's record book, it could still be wrong. Just as 'first offence' does not mean the first time you have done it but the first time you've been caught, so being a particular number on the list does not mean you deserve to be so placed. Dave Hewitt, in one of a series of articles on Munro completionists, believes there are at least nine and possibly double that number who would feature in a list of the first hundred if they had chosen to inform the Scottish Mountaineering Club of their achievement, and that a good few of the completionists are much lower in the batting order than is generally assumed.

This raises another question of why people should or should not want to see their names on a list. If

The Blackmount

it is merely the satisfaction of seeing your name in print, then pitching a half-brick through a jeweller's window would be equally effective and, more to the point, considerably cheaper. It may be that the list-ticker feels an obligation to support lists *per se*, and so ensure a compleat list of compleationists, or is merely grateful for the opportunity of a suitable epitaph to mark the termination of the eternal struggle.

Perhaps what is more interesting is why people don't own up. My own feeling was that, as the goal could be reached by anyone over the age of ten and under the age of sixty with the requisite number of limbs and sufficient determination, publicly proclaiming the feat played too easily into the hands of the Princes Street lampooners. But this may be self-deceiving. There is, it could be argued, more hubris in proclaiming yourself a non-Munroist than informing the SMC of your achievement. Perhaps, one day, there may even be a list of those who have yet to come out of the closet.

As those who are interested in lists are often also intrigued by statistics generally, the decision to go Munro-collecting offers a rich seam of opportunity. It is inherent in the activity that each success is ticked, but there is more than one way of marking this record of achievement. The committed registrars will go further than the underlining in red of their trainspotting days. The conservative will probably plump for the Church Spire Appeal approach, filling in a diagrammatic representation of the Inaccessible Pinnacle with various bands of colour to denote peaks conquered per annum. The more adventurous might use layers of shading to indicate the proportion of summer as against winter ascents. At the most ambitious end of the spectrum, opportunities are limitless, including constructing a map of Scotland with all the Munros concealed by hinged windows which, like an Advent Calendar, could in turn be opened after the appropriate moment of triumph. Electricians might even add flashing lights.

Nor is it only a matter of ticking. Various other statistics are immediately available, distance walked, time taken, verticality ascended and descended being the most obvious. On top of these are temperature and humidity readings, atmospheric pressure, calories burnt and replenished, with the relative correlation of the height and weight of the number of the party involved in any given ascent. Once all this information has been collected and analysed, it might be possible to produce a formula that, using Ben Nevis as a benchmark, would decide for once and for all the difference between a Munro and a Top. For any further deliberation as to a reorganisation of the Tables, such a 'Rule' could be invoked. This, superseding the laws of Naismith and his contemporaries, could be to modern mountaineering what Einstein was to Newtonian physics.

But, although it is important to keep a sense of proportion about the nature or value of catching a quivering Munro in the torchbeam of your self-esteem, there are a couple of serious reasons why Munro-bagging should be encouraged. Important that is, if you believe in the right for all to have access to wild country and the right for small rural communities to survive in the face of capitalist theory and practice.

At first sight, the question of access seems to pose no problem. Legislation is in place and, even without the help of the law, walkers in recent times have had little difficulty in negotiating, by one means or another, their way to the Highland summits. The place is sufficiently big and barren to accommodate the current level of visitors without too much conflict. But this must also have been true of the Lake District. Land in Scotland, and particularly that which is of interest to the climber, is owned by a relatively small number of people and these people, despite the semi-collapse of the feudal system, still have a good deal of clout. Rights can be eroded by stealth or by a combination of bureaucracy and self-serving quangos. The more people there are who have an interest in preserving the Highlands as an area of open countryside, the better.

The Munroist is particularly useful in this respect. He and she, by definition, spread the load of erosion rather than tramp up and down the overbeaten track. They can also act as an inspectorate, reporting to the relevant bodies evidence of obstruction of rights of way or other floutings of the public's entitlement. In England, even though there are many successful groups who challenge closures, it is estimated that 25% of the rights of way are not being properly maintained. A region that contains most of the British hills over 3,000 feet is even harder to police. As Munroists in their journey through the land become attuned to the impact that schemes for forestation, water supply and the like have upon it, they can add an informed voice to the debate as to whether we want, or even need, to preserve what little natural wilderness the country has left.

In the short term, the arrival of large numbers of people to walk in the hills can only be beneficial to the economy of the region. The recent closure of access caused by foot-and-mouth showed how much a rural community is dependent on visitors whose ambitions stretch above visits to the souvenir shop and boat trips round the lake. One hotelier in the Lake District commented that he would have lost less money if he had bought and slaughtered all the sheep on the surrounding fells, provided that had meant the area was free from restriction and his hotel could again welcome the walker and climber.

In the remoter areas of Scotland, the village shop and local garage will only exist if they are used. If not, they will close, the proprietors will move away. They will take their children with them, the school will close. So others move out and the second-homers, who fill up with petrol and provisions at their urban hypermarket, move in. It is the drivers who set off for the wilds of Glen Dessarry who will ensure their tanks are topped up locally and the campers returning from the wilds of Wester Ross who will replenish their rucksacks at the nearest store. Without them, all that will be left of the Highland community will be a Disneyfied version. Disneyland is not an attractive proposition, particularly if it is a land, as the graffito had it, where the disenfranchised 'disnae work, disnae care and disnae pay the bluidy poll tax'. Perhaps, after all, the humble hillwalker might indeed be the true Salvationist.

But the real reason why anyone would want to climb all the Munros must be personal to the individual. For some, it is being first – Robertson with the Munros, the Revd A R G Burn with the Tops, first continuous round, Hamish Brown and, in winter, Martin Moran. And, of course, first man to complete the round without the help of a beard, John Dow in 1933. All that is left nowadays for would-be record-breakers is to complete the round in the shortest time, which seems to be fifty-one days, or to cram as many Munros into a specified time as possible. Perhaps, in these days of continuous, if somewhat conflicting, medical advice, an underlying motive is to stay healthy or, at least, to find some incentive that will last longer than New Year resolutions. Collecting Munros is an excellent stimulus. You are unlikely to drive for several hours, perhaps even days, to bag Ben Klibreck and be put off by a bit of mist finely laced with sleet.

Nor is this a modern fad. P L J Heron, the twenty-first completionist (subject to the findings of the Hewitt Commission on Irresponsible Reticence) was well ahead of his time. In an article for the 1954 SMC Journal, entitled 'Climbing Munros Makes One Fit', he explained that, after a medical examination that pronounced him suffering from an acceleration of the normal ravages of advancing age, he was faced with the alternative of 'digging the garden in a big way or having a bash at the hills'. It took him under three years, climbing only at weekends. He put this celerity down to a reliable alarm clock and his decision to listen to the weather forecast before deciding on the day's march. As a result, more than 75% of ascents were accomplished on 'good to perfect days'. There was the added bonus that his starting point was Fort William.

He ends on a modest note, feeling that as his piece did not 'contain the descriptions of the frightful difficulties and fatal accidents usually met with in mountaineering articles' it would face editorial rejection. For, as he says, 'I am not a mountaineer.' Now if only, in addition to kissing, he had climbed to the very top of each lamp-post in Princes Street...

Torridon

Two
And the what and the wherefore

On January 10, 1889, the *Glasgow Herald* published a letter written by W N Naismith. In it he suggested the formation of a Scottish Alpine Club, membership of which would require the completion of 'a certain number of ascents either *(1)* in the Alps or *(2)* in Scotland'. The suggestion was greeted with enthusiasm, though there were reservations about the term 'Alpine'. It was thought this might mean playing second fiddle to the original – and English – version, and that as Scotland was 'one of the most mountainous countries in the world', it should stand on its own numerically superior feet. Two months later, the Scottish Mountaineering Club was duly constituted, with ninety-four original members.

What is of particular interest to the Munroist is the terms of Naismith's suggested qualification for membership. The 'Scottish version' was the ascent of six mountains over 3,500 feet. This raised the objection, appearing in the same paper four days later, that it allowed 'cheap' ascents, such as Lochnagar and Ben

Nevis, which could be visited on the back of a pony, but excluded the Cuillin, which offered the 'stiffest work in Scotland'. Naismith acquiesced, and thus the accepted height for a serious mountain became fixed at 3,000 feet. This spread across the border and the Welsh, Irish and English three-thousanders became equally sought after as a unique collection. It is, however, interesting to speculate what would have happened if the original cut-off point had been agreed and formed the basis for a definitive list of 'proper' Scottish mountains. Such a decision might have persuaded Munro to produce his Tables accordingly and this, in turn, might have altered the whole structure of peak-bagging.

A benchmark of 3,500 feet would have reduced the total Munro portfolio to less than seventy, and those 'furth' of Scotland would have been in an even sorrier state. Certainly not a target for the ardent collector or even the mountain enthusiast, excluding as it does not only the Cuillin but also many of the finest mountains in such areas as Knoydart and Torridon. Inevitably, Tables of 'Lesser Heights' would have appeared but would the collection of list upon list have had the same public appeal? In fact, the outcome might have been the encouragement of an entirely different design. As summit-bagging on a large scale only became a popular activity when road travel allowed reasonably easy approach, it might have been equally reasonable to measure the ascent not in feet above sea level, but from the highest point of acceptable vehicular access, the list being compiled to include only those hills that had 2,000 feet of 'true' ascent. Such a computation, for example, would make Elider Fawr the 'highest' mountain in Wales, rather than Snowdon. The great advantage of such a scheme is that not only would it promote some of the better, but lower-caste, Scottish hills to celebrity status (the likes of Suilven and Foinaven would be superior to a number of Naismith's

A view of the Grampians

originals, with an unvariety of dreary Mealls sinking beyond trace) but also continue to feed the on-going debate on the ethics concerning the use of ski-lifts, furnicular railways and off-road motor vehicles.

As all this is in the realms of speculation, it might be better to consider the practical problems of climbing the hills as they stand. The main mistake that the tyro-Munroist can make is to dash about with a half-formed idea of the lie of the land. It is quite easy in the euphoria of cherry-picking the summits of Kintail to realise too late that, with a little effort, you could have added Saileag to the normal round of the Five Sisters. I once omitted Toll Creagach out of pure lethargy and, for my sins, spent considerable time and effort floundering up the snow-covered slopes of one of the least prepossessing peaks in Scotland. Ron, a commited un-Munroist, who I had cajoled into a lengthy detour on our way home, was not amused.

The answer is to prepare sooner rather than later. It is a matter of sorting out your working days on the hill. This is particularly true for anyone living south of Carlisle, who has to devote a day at each end of the expedition to bashing up and down motorways. 'Haste ye back' may be the *cri d'amour* but, in planning the Munros, it is a case of more speed if less haste is expended. This in itself is not a bad thing, particularly for those who like maps and delight in logistics and see the process as less a task and more a pleasure.

There may be, on the other hand, those with so much time and money on their hands that they choose to leave the odd summit or two scattered about as an excuse to return in due course, but I was not one of them. My particular nemesis was a round above Glenshee which included Carn Aosda, The Cairnwell, Carn a' Gheoidh and An Socach. It was a good day and I returned to the valley well satisfied with my efforts. It was only then I discovered my error. The District Guide that I had been using was rather old and followed the one-inch OS map, which had the summit as Socach Mor at 3,073 feet – and that was the point I had reached. Resurveying had changed matters and the highest point was currently the previous Top, situated a mile or so to the west at the other end of the ridge and now deemed twenty feet higher. As it had not formed part of my route of ascent or descent, I had not even had the luck to do it accidentally. My companion, who had declined the opportunity of the extra peak on the grounds that it was an unnecessary extension to the day, and thus reached the comforts of civilisation some considerable time before me, found the whole affair rather amusing.

Assuming you have read the correct map correctly, there is usually little problem in locating the summit cairn. It is more often than not just a question of keeping going up until there is no more up to go. But there is first the little matter of setting foot on the hill itself. Unlike England, where the ground is covered by a criss-cross of tracks of every dimension, the Scottish hills are relatively pathless. Yet, because starting points suggested by convenient parking are commonly used, there is often evidence of a minor trail setting off in the direction of your chosen peak. You stride along this confidently, but sooner or later – and it's usually sooner – it starts to waver and then disappears altogether. The truth is that, so far, even the most determined efforts by mankind to beat the vegetation into submission have failed. The nature of the ground is sufficiently rough and waterbound that all are forced to pick their own path to avoid the worst of the terrain and, once well away from the road, it is not impossible that you are stepping on a bit of land that no human has ever stepped on before. In addition, the Highlands are so often covered in snow that the already resilient heath is protected in a manner that does not occur in the more southerly parts of Britain. The paths that do exist are for the most part man-made for stalking or removing the deceased deer from the hill. They are very useful where they exist but rarely, as there is little point, finish on a summit or necessarily travel in the required Munro-direction. Nevertheless, any alleviation from the ankle-trapping heather is to be welcomed and if a path is marked on the map it is always worth considering.

But for every plus in life there is a minus. The paths exist because of the deer forest and the deer forest exists to keep outsiders as well as stags at bay. The current political thinking is that wild land should be open to all. However, as a parallel example, the abolition of hunting with dogs has yet to become universally accepted and those who feel similarly hard done-by, at this particular turn of their wheel, may refuse to co-operate and, instead, mobilise their forces to safeguard their perceived legal rights. A meeting of the Scottish Countryside Alliance in 2003 threw up just such a case. Sir Iain Noble, founder of the Noble Grossart merchant bank and owner of an estate on Skye, suggested that the English should be prevented from settling on the island to preserve the island's genetic purity. He explained that he wasn't against foreigners (indeed, some of his most influential friends probably fell into that category) but not in his own backyard, setting up what he described as 'ghettos.' Although the Alliance completely dissociated itself from Sir Iain's views, it is likely he was talking, at least in part, to a sympathetic audience.

The essence of the law is that open and wild land should be available to all, but land designated for domestic, commercial and recreational activities (for example, golf) should be immune to public access. In England this could mean that islands of moorland could well exist on which the public have the right to roam but are unable to reach, except by helicopter. In Scotland, because of the expanse of open countryside and the much lower level of exempted human activity, this is less likely. But it does not mean there is less of a threat. There is not the network of rights of way in Scotland that exists south of the border and it would not be that difficult for landowners to make access to the hill, if not impossible, at least very inconvenient. I am not suggesting that they would go to the extent of surrounding a selection of significant mountains with twenty-four hour golf courses, but there has recently been a suggestion that a substantial area be fenced off to allow the reintroduction of wolves and the like.

There already exists the legitimate locking of gates to prevent vehicular access to a convenient starting or finishing point. The most obvious example is at Struy, where permission has to be gained from the nearby cottage if you wish to drive down Glen Strathfarrar. To be able to do this makes the possibility of completing the Farrar Four in one outing much more feasible. My experience of this was that permission was given somewhat grudgingly, and without any leeway if you overran the strictly enforced time limit. In a society that still has a tendency to doff the cap, it is quite easy for those with the ability to control circumstance and so manipulate the situation to their advantage. Locked gates, overseen by various jobsworths, may spring up where none had been before.

So, from access to ethics. To complete the Munros, you must effect an ascent of each tabulated summit. But what constitutes a proper ascent of a mountain? Clearly, reaching the top – but from what point of departure? A Munro is a hill over 3,000 feet above sea level but, with few exceptions, it would be absurd to assume that a true ascent would cover every vertical inch. On the other hand, taking the chairlift virtually to the summit of The Cairnwell would certainly be regarded as cheating. Would taking the chairlift down also rule out a proper ascent? Must you walk up *and* down and, if so, where does glissading fit into the equation? Hamish Brown, when planning his continuous walk around all the Munros, decided that any form of human propulsion was permissible, which enabled him to cycle and, on one occasion, canoe from one mountain group to another. So does that mean you can cycle to the summit and hang-glide back to your car?

A Knoydart seascape

Probably not worth the effort. A friend of mine, a keen cyclist, wished to journey from Aviemore to Braemar. On his cycle-touring map there appeared to be a shortcut delineated through the heart of the Cairngorms. The Lairig Ghru is an old drove road and, as such, well trodden by man and beast. However, it is not designed for bikes and if the weather turns is, as some have discovered to their cost, a dangerous place. The summit of the pass is nearly 3,000 feet high and there is little in the way of shelter. Luckily, the weather held and the crossing was made without undue incident. However, I was led to understand that the type of apparel that is conducive for efficient cycling leaves something to be desired when struggling up and down a badly eroded path with a bike around your neck.

It could be argued that the proper way to complete an ascent of the hills in Munro's Tables is to do it under similar conditions of transport, that is, using the rail system, boat and bicycle, as were available to the originator. Sir Hugh recalls in the SMC Journal that it was perfectly feasible to catch the early morning train from Glasgow, spend a day in the hills around Loch Ossian and continue to Fort William for dinner. In fact, such an outing is equally feasible today, but the Beeching axe in the 1950s has severely limited similar such possibilities for the modern explorer. There were, in addition, other advantages open to Sir Hugh and his fellow travellers. Having a private yacht at your disposal is a distinct plus when visiting the hills that surround the lochs of Nevis and Hourn, and during his longer stravaigs he could count on finding accommodation in the most remote of areas. Buildings now ruined were the homes of shepherds and the like who were only too willing to exchange a bed for the latest news and a taste of Edinburgh whisky. But, in the absence of any final arbiter on the subject, it must be assumed that, in the end, it is a case of each to his or her own conscience. Queen Victoria, I understand, used to take to the hill in some sort of customised barouche.

But what has to be accepted about the Scottish hills and most distinguishes them from their more comfortable southern cousins is the weather. There is no shortage of low cloud and mist in the Lake District but the consequences of going astray are not as serious as in much of the Highlands. If you find yourself in the wrong Scottish glen through navigational error, you could be a very long walk from any sort of habitation, let alone your desired destination.

The possibility of this once happened to me when walking in the Drumochter hills. I had been dropped at the head of the pass and intended to walk over A' Bhuidheanach Bheag and Carn na Caim back to Dalwhinnie.

This is a featureless piece of land and was covered with thick mist, which necessitated some careful map and compass work. My Silva compass had seen better days and chose this moment for the needle to become detached from its fulcrum and lie, a disconsolate derelict, at the bottom of its housing. Fortunately, through vigorous shaking, I persuaded it to re-balance and swing towards the appropriate direction. Of course, with any sudden movement it fell off again and more juggling had to take place. I can only attribute my somewhat laboured success to the hours spent as a child attempting to master an infuriating toy where you had to manoeuvre a number of miniature ballbearings into a series of indentations in the base of a perspex box. As today's equivalent training would be hours spent on the latest version of PlayStation, my advice to the young is at all times to carry a spare compass, no matter how rudimentary in nature.

Then there is the rain. Again, a common enough

mountain phenomenon, but in Scotland there is an added dimension. Crossing unbridged rivers and streams is the normal part of a day's outing and a vigorous downpour can change a gentle paddle into something much more serious. I was with a small party staying at the bothy in Glen Beg. We had completed a round of the Beinn Dearg group of Munros and, returning to the bothy, had to cross the Allt Uisg a' Bhrisdidh, a stream that was so dry that we didn't get our feet wet. That night it rained. The next day we had to recross the Allt on our way back to Ullapool. By this time it was too deep to ford without swimming, so I decided the prudent decision was to climb back up the hillside until matters eased. Because the land fell steeply at this point, the stream was really a staircase of waterfalls with fast-running foam for each riser and a series of deep but equally fast-running pools for each tread. To try to wade the pools ran the risk of being swept over a fall, to cross the foam ensured that you were, so we were faced with what turned out to be a 1,000ft climb to to find a safe crossing.

And, finally, there is snow. There scarcely seems a month in the year when snow cannot fall in the Highlands. I spent my honeymoon in August bat-

Ben Lawers

tling against blizzards on the Cuillin. In fact, though
the calendar might have indicated that I climbed
the majority of the Munros during the more clem-
ent parts of the year, over a fifth of the ascents were
sufficiently wintry to merit carrying an ice axe. The
worst white-out I have experienced happened on an
autumn day. Again, I had been dropped at the head
of the Drumochter Pass, to be picked up at Dalwhinnie. On this occasion, the hills of choice lay to the
west side of the A9, overlooking Loch Ericht. A heavy
fall had drifted on the eastern slopes of Sgairneach
Mhor and, having trudged through knee-deep soft
snow, I was grateful when the land began to level off
on to the summit plateau. But not for long. I had previously been sheltered from the wind. Now, exposed
to its full force, I was surrounded by swirling snow
that reduced visibility to zero.

I was separated from my next objective, Beinn
Udlamain, by a drop of some 500 feet that landed on

a somewhat indeterminate-looking watershed. The problem I faced was that if I misjudged the length of the descent and, as is easily done, followed the line of least resistance, I could have ended up in entirely the wrong valley to my left. The easiest solution would have been to compensate by trending right, but a band of serious-looking cliffs ran along the edge of the plateau. At least, these were the facts according to the map. My own observation was limited to a more than passable imitation of the opening credits of *Dr Who*. In these conditions it is difficult to judge distances, particularly the depth of a sudden drop in the ground. On more than one occasion, what appeared from above as a fathomless abyss turned out after some trepidation to be no more than a gentle undulation. My instinct and compass were at odds and I had to remind myself, sometimes quite forcibly, that the compass doesn't lie.

Eventually I stopped going downhill and was, I hoped, at the watershed. If I could find evidence of streams flowing both north and south, I would know where I was but, of course, the wind had frozen all possible clues. I had no alternative but to assume I was right and started to climb with some trepidation towards the supposed shoulder of Beinn Udlamain.

When doubts were at their height, I luckily walked into a fence post and knew all was well. The map showed a regional boundary of some sort that followed my intended route for the next couple of miles to the third Munro, A' Mharconaich, and if things didn't get better by then, it would be easy enough to drop down on to the stalkers' path that led to Balsporran Cottages, with the possibility of thumbing a lift to Dalwhinnie.

But whatever it was that had decided to amuse itself at the sight of my flounderings must have tired of the game, for the front passed through, to be replaced by clear blue skies. The line of posts marching into the distance became superfluous. I let go of its hand and stopped to look back on my odyssey – a sloping hillside running gently up to some rather scattered lumps of rock. Much ado about not a lot.

With careful organisation and good luck, all the above hazards can be avoided by the aspirant Munroist. The Cuillin cannot.

Three
Skye's the limit

Although the Munros of the Cuillin are scattered throughout the Table, they still exist as a sub-set, part of the whole, yet physically and mentally distinct. This is the challenge within a challenge that the average hillwalker must weigh up if he or she is to trouble the Keeper of the List. A glance at the relevant section of the Tables gives the game away. *Sgurrs* to the left of you, *Sgurrs* to the right of you, and it requires only a smattering of the local vernacular to know that *Sgurr* translates as a peak that is dramatically pointed, and 'dramatically pointed' means that some climbing skill may well be required. The roll call must cause some concern among those particular aspirants who would prefer others to clean the windows of their bungalow rather than do it themselves.

Nor does the name of the ridge, at large, help to dispel the concern. The Norse *Kjölen* means like the 'keel of a boat' and/or 'ridge of mountains' and is the likely origin of the modern Cuillin. This does not seem too bad until you remember that the mountain scenery of Norway bears little resemblance to that of the South Downs. Alternatively, the Celtic word *Coolin* means 'worthless'. This, of course, is as seen from the viewpoint of those trying to eke a living out of the land, rather than that of the well-off Victorian mountaineer. The only worthless piece of ground to the impoverished is barren rock and that usually means slabs of stone in an exposed and steep location. The fairy-tales do not soften the blow. Cuchullain, the hero of the Gael, was believed, among his other trials of strength and prowess, to have walked across the 'bridge of cliffs'. This was supposedly some part of the Cuillin, possibly the Pinnacle Ridge of Sgurr nan Gillean, and the legend leaves no doubt as to the enormity of the task.

Even when the tourists arrived, the press didn't improve. Dr Johnson's view was that 'A walk upon ploughed fields in England is a dance upon carpets compared to the toilsome drudgery of walking in Skye' and he got nowhere *near* the mountains. It wasn't until Sir Walter Scott landed at Loch Scavaig and walked into Coruisk that matters changed. The sight he saw inspired his poem 'The Lord of the Isles', which in turn attracted popular attention to this remote part of the island. Boatloads landed, guidebooks proliferated and Turner painted. So, did Skyeboat-flummery begin. But it was nearly a quarter of a century after the visit from the Wizard of the North that the first 'Munro' (Sgurr nan Gillean) was climbed by a forester, Duncan MacIntyre, and Professor James Forbes.

MacIntyre had already made a significant foray into the range in the previous year. He had guided the Revd C Lessingham Smith into Coruisk via Glen Sligachan and was sufficiently impressed with Smith's ability to suggest a shortcut home over Druim nan Ramh. Smith, trusting in his gentleman's alpenstock, the umbrella, agreed and made the first

Cuchullain's 'bridge of cliffs'

Cuillin scramble on record. Other guides were not so adventurous and, as with many of their Alpine counterparts, preferred the route they knew rather than to stray from the narrow path. Professor Knight had to bribe his courier to traverse from the summit of Sgurr nan Gillean to his eponymous peak at the top of the Pinnacle Ridge. The reluctant 'second' was so shaken by the experience that he refused to accompany Knight on a planned three-day expedition that would involve the use of a rope.

Such use was, in fact, revolutionary in these parts. Alexander Nicolson, initially guided by the son of Duncan MacIntyre, made the first ascent of a significant number of peaks without one. Perhaps the most impressive of these was the successful attempt on Sgurr Dubh Mor, starting on a late September afternoon. He and a friend reached the summit at sunset and decided to take the shortest descent available into Coir' an Lochain. This culminated in a series of steep walls which are still regarded as a bit of a challenge, even by people carrying the appropriate gear. Unflustered, Nicolson unwound a plaid rug he always carried with him. His companion held one end while Nicolson slithered down to the other. Then, with reverse combined tactics, he would catch the lighter man as he dropped at arm's length from the ledge above. This method might upset the purists, yet Nicolson was a man before his time: in 1872 he suggested a bridge to connect the Kyle of Lochalsh with Kyleakin.

But by the time the present-day Munroists arrive at the scene, they will feel that the spadework has been done. There is no longer any mystery and little loose rock. The only thing they are likely to be bombarded with is their own misgivings. It is still a complex piece of topography but has been well documented. J Wilson Parker's *Scrambles in Skye* is not the falsely modest title of some early explorer's account of hanging on by his eyebrows, but a detailed account of approach paths, convenient points of access and the various ways of attaining the chosen summit. It also describes the connecting pieces of the ridge so that the summits can be linked together in a series of high-level traverses.

Each route is graded for the walker/scrambler, with the lowest being hands-in-pockets and the highest the climbing grade of Very Difficult. Thus, the scale progresses from walking through scrambling to the easier end of rock climbing. Even so, this assessment must be subjective as it is difficult to say when scrambling stops and rock climbing begins. It could be said that if you use your hands merely to speed up propulsion or assist balance you are still scrambling, but when the arms become necessary to ensure either of the above motor activities, then climbing has started. Before you set off, it is probably important to distinguish the difference and find out for yourself where your personal line lies.

When I first started climbing, a friend and I, by chance, stayed at a farmhouse run by Scotty Dwyer, who was one of the few professional guides operating in Britain. His advice and library were invaluable to our climbing education, as was the instance when we first saw him in action. It was on the Slabs. He had taken his party up Tennis Shoes, while we floundered around on one of Idwal's holy trinity. Once up, he must have felt it prudent to check on his paying guests and diagonally descended to the point where we were belayed. After a quick (and kindly) word, he walked back up to his clients. I say 'walked' as it is the only word that can be used in the light of my above definition. He didn't seem to use his hands for any real climbing purpose and his ease of movement showed he was a man who had never 'scrambled' in his life.

By Parker's definition, only Am Basteir, Sgurr Dearg and Sgurr Mhic Coinnich require rock-climbing skills if the summits are to be reached, but to take the easiest route available is often to miss the point. The best bet for the Munro-bagger is to get up and stay up. You might not be able to do the lot in one day, but it is quite possible to do it in three, or at most four expeditions. The alternative of picking them off one by one is not that enthralling, particularly if it means flogging up the likes of The Great Stone Shoot of Sgurr Alasdair on each occasion.

Moving from south to north, the first section is bounded by the Thearlaich Dubh Gap, which is the most formidable obstacle on the ridge that cannot be avoided. So it is best to take Sgurr nan Eag and Sgurr Dubh Mor as a separate pair. Although it is easy enough to approach this section of the ridge from Glen Brittle, it would be the ideal opportunity to start from the east side of the ridge and explore Loch Coruisk and its environ. It is a fair walk in and it would probably be better to camp, provided you can avoid the most-midge months. The routes are the 'Shore Path' from Glen Brittle, the long haul from Sligachan, or via the not-so-Bad Step from Elgol. The latter obstacle was formerly known as

Ceum Carach – The Ladies' Step – though whether this is a reflection of their neatness of movement or supposed pusillanimity is not quite clear.

The middle section are the peaks that surround Coire Lagan, Sgurr Alasdair, Sgurr Mhic Coinnich and Sgurr Dearg, the traverse of which forms a classic cirque. It is easy enough to add Sgurr na Banachdich and, if going well, the additional Munros of Sgurr a' Ghreadaidh and Sgurr a' Mhadaidh. However, the necessary crossing of the subsidiary Top of Sgurr Thearlaich and Sgurr Mhic Coinnich by either Collie's Ledge or King's Chimney is at the upper end of Parker's scale and, if coupled with the Inaccessible Pinnacle that forms the summit of Sgurr Dearg, may be considered more than enough for one day.

The final section contains both the most accessible of the Cuillin Munros, Bruach na Frithe, and probably the most photographed, Sgurr nan Gillean. In between lies the ominously named Am Basteir, the Executioner. This is not as bad as it sounds, as the east ridge is relatively straightforward and the cautious collector will be relieved that its Tooth at 3,005 feet is only a Top rather than a separate mountain. If all three Munros are to be done as one, it will also involve the West Ridge of Sgurr nan Gillean before the Tourist Route leads back to Sligachan. A better but more difficult way would be to travel in the opposite direction. This would enable the climber to follow Cuchullain's footsteps and reach the top of Sgurr nan Gillean by the renowned Pinnacle Ridge. Apart from the descent from the top of the Third Pinnacle to the gap between it and Knight's Peak, there are no especial difficulties and that *mauvais pas* could always be abseiled.

For the ambitious Munroist, the proper challenge would be the traverse of the ridge in one journey. As this would include eleven Munros in an outing, it would, in every way, put the South Glen Shiel Ridge with its seven Munros into a considerable shade. At a casual glance, the expeditions look similar. The Kintail Ridge involves a journey of fifteen miles and the ascent of 17,500 feet, the Cuillin Ridge fifteen and 10,000. If Naismith were to apply his formula, the day in Kintail would take between three and four hours longer than the Traverse of the Main Ridge. But Naismith knew enough about the Cuillin to make it the exception to his rule.

The difficulties involved necessarily mean that movement will be slower on Skye than when strid-

The Cuillin Ridge from the west

ing around the Monadh Liath. Norman Collie, the mountaineer most associated with the second phase of Cuillin exploration, took eighteen hours to explore the central section of the ridge that lies between Sgurr a' Mhadaidh and Sgurr Thearlaich and, with that in mind, it was thought impossible, even given Scottish summer daylight, to complete the ridge in one go. It was certainly no place on which to be wandering about in the dark. But ambitions in the climbing world were changing. Prodigious feats of walking were being performed in the Lake District. A W Wakefield had linked together all the major Cumbrian summits in under twenty-four hours, clocking up over 23,000 feet in the process. Of course, Skye was a different matter but people began to consider it a possibility.

The matter was much debated and the basis of the debate had been laid down by the Abraham brothers in their book on climbing in Skye. In their opinion, if there was to be any chance of success, there must be a combination of three essential elements – an exceptionally strong and neat climber who knew the ridge intimately, an outing blessed with kind weather and a 'carefully arranged commissariat'. The first is self-evident. It would be a long day and any over-reliance on the hands would result in them being 'torn to pieces before he had got halfway'. (Before the introduction of DNA testing a friend of mine once ruefully remarked that a week on gabbro was a prerequisite for anyone wishing to commit the perfect crime.)

The next requirements are also obvious, as speed is of the essence and you don't want to spend time studying maps. And it is particularly true if the mist comes down. Unlike in the rest of Scotland, you will find that your compass does lie and at a series of critical moments local conditions can override Magnetic North. Even C D Frankland, arguably the best climber in Britain at the time, could not find his way from Sgurr Dearg to Bealach Coire na Banachdich. Seven times he tried and seven times he failed, until at last he was forced to beat an ignominious retreat whence he had come. The Ridge is not a single track but a confusion of branch lines and even in good visibility the proper way is not always obvious.

Abraham's final point is particularly significant. There is no running water on the ridge (F S Smythe and J H B Bell took a length of rubber hose to enable them to syphon off any incipient rock pools) and the usual practice is to cache some water *en route*. My own experience of this is somewhat chequered. We dutifully carried a largish container of water to the Bealach na Glaic Moire, which we considered the optimum point to alleviate dehydration. On our later arrival we found that it had disappeared from behind the unmistakably configured rock formation that had hidden it from view. I drew the obvious conclusion – reparation for past wrongs by the Sassenach, etc.

At least, until a couple of decades later, when I laced together a sponsored walk/run across the watershed from Coniston Old Man to the top of Skiddaw. During days of preliminary reconnaissance I had secreted small bottles of a mineral-based liquid at various points on the route. The potion was not pleasant and over-indulgence tended to have the same effect as chewing sandpaper but it was supposed to replace vital salts *et al* and had been earnestly recommended by a man with a degree in veterinary science. I also took the precaution of burying a can of beer under a pile of rubble. As matters turned out, I was only able to retrieve one item of the trove. This particular item I had hidden in a U-shaped burrow on the Langdale Pikes that looked as if it had been constructed by an oversized and geographically confused lugworm. Inevitably, it was not the beer. The rest had disappeared (border raiders) or possibly the 'unmistakably configured rock(s)' weren't quite what they seemed.

Eventually the deed was done. In 1911 Leslie Shadbolt and Alistair MacLaren completed the ridge, starting from Glen Brittle and finishing at Sligachan in sixteen and three-quarter hours. T H Somervell repeated the task, finishing the second half of the ridge alone, and in 1924 B R Goodfellow and F Yates of the Rucksack Club climbed the ridge the more difficult way from north to south. Around the same time, the Pinnacle Club, an all-women's climbing club, took an interest in the challenge. They were camped at Loch Scavaig and intended to attack the ridge from the inside of the horseshoe. If successful, this would achieve two precedents, ie the first complete traverse by a woman and the first expedition to start and finish at the same point. Their plan was overtaken by others and Mabel Barker (although she later became a member of the club) achieved the proposed feat in August 1926, accompanied by C D Frankland.

B H Humble in his *The Cuillin of Skye* (a *Neate* starred classic published by Hale in 1952) noted 'that they kept strictly to the ridge and did not carry a rope which reveals a very high standard of climbing and endurance on the part of the female member of the party.' Perhaps he was unaware that a year earlier the same party had completed the fourth ascent of Central Buttress on Scafell, then regarded as the hardest climb in Britain and amongst the hardest in the world. Nor was it the case that the 'female member' had merely been towed up. The difficult traverses above the Flake required equal skill from both partners and Barker herself led the final section of the Flake.

Humble compounds his act of patronising disparagement by suggesting that now a woman had done the traverse, the men naturally lost interest. Yet, at another moment, he displays sympathy for two later male parties who were forced to drop out at the last hurdle. He rounded off this historical appraisal by demonstrating that the ridge had slid down the scale from 'Impossible' to an 'Easy Day for a Lady', with the observation that 'Dorothy Hudson, a young girl of seventeen with but three months climbing experience, accomplished it without much difficulty' and – the crowning insult – she did it wearing hiking shorts. I suppose, in a way, he was right. Mabel Barker, even at the age of seventeen, might have found it, compared to some, easy enough.

Probably the average Munroist would not choose to apply that particular epithet to this section of the Grand Tour and, if not a rock climber, would be wise to seek expert advice. The Cuillin is rarely straightforward but comfort can be gained in the knowledge that even the great Collie failed on his first two attempts to set foot on the ridge and had eventually to be shepherded up the Tourist Route by John MacKenzie. This need for 'a man who knows' is especially true when it comes to climbing the Inaccessible Pinnacle.

The summit of Sgurr Dearg is anything but inaccessible, as a visit on a fine summer's day will testify. But it must have appeared so to the Admiralty surveyors, at least as a potential site for a trig point. Nevertheless, it was this nomenclature that attracted the attention of the Pilkington brothers, who were tempted to interrupt a fishing trip in the Hebrides in 1880 to see for themselves. Lawrence recalls many years later in an article for the SMC Journal (1939) that it was 'the noisiest climb I ever had'. The rock that formed the narrow edge of the pinnacle had been shattered by the elements to such an extent that he and his brother had to peel off a foot or so of the top surface, hurling the offending pieces to the ground below as they proceeded to the summit. 'The noise was appalling; the very rock of the pinnacle itself seemed to vibrate with indignation at our rude assault.' They and their successors must have done a pretty thorough job, for when Pilkington returned three years later there was not 'a single loose rock on the ridge'.

Nowadays, the problem for non-climbers is not getting up, for, though exposed, the east ridge provides no more difficulty than many other parts of the gabbro backbone. Indeed, if Bidein Druim nan Ramh had been 150 feet higher, it, rather than the Pinnacle, might have proved to be the 'worst step' of all. The greater problem is getting down. The usual practice is to abseil, but that means we are back to ski-lifts. There is very little difference between sliding

The In Pinn

down a rope and being pulled up one. At the time of its first ascent, there was a debate as to whether it was sporting to use a rope at all when climbing in the Cuillin, and the Visitors' Book in the Sligachan Hotel bore vigorous testimony. H C Hart, a botanist from Dublin, poured scorn on the precautions taken by others and, after making the first continuous round of Coire Lagan, including a west–east traverse of the In Pinn, made it clear in his account that no ropes had been used at any time. An addendum by another guest suggested, 'A rope with a noose at the end and a long drop would have suited this idiot.'

As pinnacles go, it does not compare in difficulty with Napes Needle. Haskett Smith, who made the first ascent of the latter, thought little of its Scottish equivalent, climbing up and down the east ridge in ten minutes, observing that care rather than skill was the real necessity and, as he didn't rope off the top of the Needle, he might well have argued that a proper bagging of a summit requires the climber to climb both up and down. However, this presents its own problems. To return by the easiest route is usually not possible unless you are prepared to crawl over the upward-moving elevator of human beings. In which case, the only way down is the steeper west ridge, which even Haskett Smith would have to concede requires some technical ability.

In winter, you would probably have the place to yourself but that can also produce difficulties. Martin Moran, when making the first winter ascent of the Munros as a continuous journey, arrived at the foot of the climb equipped with only a rope and a couple of old slings to allow a classic abseil. Without any hardware, not even karabiners, he was back with the pioneers, with the exception that the summer Moderate was now 'at least a Grade III winter route'. (For an account of how the best of climbers can get into sub-zero difficulties, Tom Patey's article in the 1965 SMC Journal on the first winter Traverse is both amusing and instructive.) It is likely therefore that, if the original dictum that the ascent and descent must be achieved 'without the use of ropes or other illegitimate means' had come into force, it would have significantly reduced the number of names forwarded to the Keeper of the List.

What is particularly thought-provoking is what would have happened if the protuberance in question had been situated not on Sgurr Dearg but on Ben Nevis. It is hard to believe that the highest point in Britain would be denied to the general public. One assumes that staircases would have been constructed, balusters fixed and safety rails placed around the summit-viewing station. There would probably have been an entry fee and itinerant candy-floss sellers. I imagine both Sir Hugh and noble Sir Iain would have had something to say about that. Though they could take comfort in the knowledge that human erosion would in due course cut the offending obelisk down to size.

Four
Bothies, bivouacs and British Rail

There is no doubt that the easiest way to tackle the Munros is with a Campervan – and there are those who would argue that it is the best. You can get yourself in pole position and probably find yourself first on the hill. This not only allows you to see golden eagles, pine martens and the like, but also frees you from any timetable imposed by others. Circumstances dictated that my regular autumnal visit to Scotland, courtesy of just such a vehicle, usually began over the weekend when the clocks went back. If we had been standard Bed & Breakfasters, we would inevitably have lost an hour of daylight. So, for the week in question, we chose to ignore the diktats of Greenwich and continued as before, extending Summer Time for a further seven days. Of course, it meant getting back to the pub awfully early, but we did get the eventual lie-in when it was really needed.

I suppose, therefore, that the next logical step for the Munroist-in-a-hurry is the 4x4 Dormobile.

If equipped with the appropriately constructed bull-bars, it could crash through locked gates and career up landrover tracks to within feet of the summit. I am not sure that this is what the legislature had in mind when it produced its Land Reform Act, but maybe it should have considered the direction of travel of our must-have-now capitalist society. A society that was less born than 'untimely ripped' by financial institutions eager to exploit the usury market. The slogan ran *Take the Waiting out of Wanting* and, curiously enough, its piece of magic plastic chanced to be called ACCESS.

The coup de disgrace would be the off-road, all-terrain machine, the ultimate in SUVs. At the moment it is difficult to tell in which sport these vehicles are supposedly useful, at least within the OED definition of the term, 'amusement esp. of the outdoor or athletic kind'. In my experience, taking children to school may offer a degree of gymnastics but is rarely amusing. Enthusiasts might argue there is a sporting element in acquiring a mixed bag of hedgehogs, watervoles and weasels, with perhaps even the odd hare, as they plough the beaten track through the groves of academe – but not with much conviction.

In–tro–du–cing **SleepaTank**

Faster than the Average Fox!!!

Now, that's a very different kettle of mammals. Who needs dogs when you can run 'em over?

So perhaps the Munroists who have chosen areas of peace and beauty rather than the pavements of Princes Street from which to gather their assemblage of beacons should consider their responsibilities before unnecessarily polluting the atmosphere. I have always been vaguely unsure about motor cars. I suppose being knocked over by one as a small child didn't help. They seem to attract a degree of significance that is often entirely out of proportion to their function. What other piece of machinery has been the butt of such pitiless jokes as those that have fallen on the hapless Lada or, in shinier translations, been portrayed as an over-elaborate trap to ensnare attractive young women?

As the chapter title suggests, and as I have pointed out elsewhere, there is an alternative. It is possible to construct a less polluting plan of campaign that has all the mountain-climbing advantages of the camper-van, albeit without the sybaritic convenience. A good example of this would be an expedition into the mountain area that lies between Loch Eil and Loch Hourn. This area, comprising the best bits of

Knoydart, is arguably one of the finest parts of Scotland and was known to the Outdoor Sections of the broadsheets as the Whitbread Wilderness, owned as it once was by the manufacturer of that variety of a palatable hops-and-malt hash. In the 1980s there was much anxiety that the area would be taken over as a training ground for those entrusted to bring democracy to the unenlightened, and that climbers, who previously had only endured the wrath of high velocity rifles, would now face much heavier ordnance. The Sundays carried emotive photographs of sturdy chaps, wreathed in the smoke of ropes and pipe tobacco, surveying this particular version of the Celtic Twilight from their chosen eyries. The readership was left to imagine the lament on the pipes for itself.

However, wiser counsels prevailed, or perhaps the money ran out, and the threat receded. Indeed, such schemes of military aggrandisement would be difficult to resurrect in the present climate of access for all and in the presence of the practical steps taken towards social ownership by the likes of the John Muir Trust. So it can be assumed that any plan for camping and climbing in the area can be carried out unmolested. The strategy would be to leave the train at Glenfinnan. Then spend as many days as it takes, or you have spare, before boarding it once more at Mallaig. In four or five days you could collect all the Munros in this pretty inaccessible area.

An early start from Bonnie Prince Charlie's Monument would take in Sgurr nan Coireachan and Sgurr Thuilm before dropping down into Glen Dessarry and stopping overnight in the bothy at A' Chuil. The next day another Sgurr nan Coireachan (the replication of name shows the separateness of the glens) can be gained, which allows a fine ridge walk over Garbh Chioch Mhor to the imposing Sgurr na Ciche. Thence via the Coire na Ciche to pick up the stalkers' path that leads to Loch Nevis and Sourlies, one of the best, if smaller, bothies in Scotland. The next day treads the Rough Bounds of Knoydart over Meall Buidhe and Luinne Bheinn to Barrisdale and Loch Hourn. The final outing is a fitting conclusion, a round of Ladhar Bheinn before descending to Inverie to catch the ferry to Mallaig.

But this is the ticker's route. If, as in *Desert Island Discs*, I could take one Munro memory other than the Bible (An Teallach) and Shakespeare (Liathach) it would be OS Map 33, Loch Alsh and Glen Shiel. The region it covers represents much of what is best in the Scottish Highlands. The map encompasses an area in excess of six hundred square miles of mountainous landscape (thirty-four Munros, nineteen Corbetts, eleven Grahams) with a significant amount of freshwater and sea lochs. Through the whole of this space there is but one thoroughfare, the A87. Apart from this, the most escapist of highways (aka The Road to the Isles), a couple of single-track roads nudge in from the east and another eases around the coastline of Loch Duich and Maxwell's rings of bright water. Each comes to an abrupt halt. Campervanners are advised to check their fuel gauges.

It is true that the A890 sneaks into the top left-hand corner but this is less an intrusion, more an exit strategy through the back of another wardrobe into Life-After-Munro Land, with its vignettes of sculptured castles and more delicate peninsulas. Map 33 has broader brush-strokes – deeply riven glens that ride up to the watershed before spilling themselves into outstretched stubby fingers that clutch the sea. Mountains where you can look down on eagles and, if it is Sgurr nan Ceathreamhnan, most of the Highland hills that you have climbed or are ever likely to. Of habitation there is little, only names to mark the cartographical coincidence of what has been and what by now remains.

'What has been and what by now remains'

If you are to explore this and similar areas, rather than just rush through them, you will need to stay, and for that all climbers in Scotland should be grateful for the efforts of the Mountain Bothies Association. Over the years, its members have rescued, renovated and repaired a number of remote buildings that otherwise would probably have been destroyed by the elements. Some were former dwellings, others simple shelters for shepherds, ghillies and the like, who had to spend some continuous time on the hill. This transformation was due to and typical of much of the free time and labour that contributed to the culture of amateur sport and recreation which characterised British life in the last century. Sad to say, this form of national service seems to be less with us and has been further discouraged by a more stringent approach to Health & Safety and Child Protection. Though not to gainsay the merits of, and indeed need for, such legislation, it seems absurd that a rock-climbing instructor should be subjected to the same codes of practice as a roofer. What is worse is that the volunteer, tired of coping with endless red tape, may well give up.

It is for this reason that I feel that Munroists should consider their collective responsibility and, at least, become paid-up members of the MBA. Even if they choose not to use the shelters for overnight accommodation, they might welcome their existence if matters turn for the worse. Common sense would suggest that, as there are more people trying to complete the round, there will be more accidents. The existence of a convenient refuge could make all the difference to both rescuers and rescued. Nor would the progression simply be arithmetic. There are several reasons why the growth of disaster could be exponential if we assume that a greater proportion of the hopefuls were to come from south of the border.

Such hillwalkers may be experienced in finding their way round the Lake District during the summer months and assume the Highlands are more of the same. But, as mentioned before, winter conditions are never far away and to find yourself on a wind-hardened snow slope without an axe can be an unfortunate experience, particularly if a gentle slide leads to a more vertical descent. And there is rather more rock in Scotland that cannot be so easily avoided. Much of it is easy enough when dry, not so when wet, particularly when the wet becomes solid. Craig Caldwell, a climber sufficiently experienced to complete the first continuous journey around the Munros and Corbetts, had to re-jig his schedule because of ice on the top few feet of The Cobbler. As a final coffin-nailer, if time and money have already been spent, prudence may not always prevail.

But the worst would be if Munro-gathering became the same sort of sponsored 'challenge' as bungee-jumping. It is not difficult to imagine the possible outcome of an announcement by the Berkshire Society for the Protection of Cruelty to Pigeons that, to celebrate its Golden Jubilee and fund its latest loft conversion, it intended to place a member (and pigeon) on the summit of fifty separate Munros at exactly the same time on a given day.

All welcome from 8 to 80. First home wins.

Forms available from Hon Sec, etc.

As well as a refuge for the injudicious, bothies are often worth visiting for their own sakes. There can be few better settings for a brew than Shenavall. There may be other places in the world where the feeling of isolation brought about by a combination of stretching water and encircling mountains can be bettered, but not many within an easy walk from a road. Several have their own history and charm – Ben Alder Cottage with its resident ghost, or Resourie with its incumbent polecat. Some, like the latter and the Teahouse, are secluded and not easy to find until you see a chimney poking through the trees. Others, like Maol Bhuidhe, stand defiant of the wilderness like another good deed in a naughty world. There is no better or easier way of exploring the Cuillin of Rum than from the bothy at Dibidil, or the north-west tip of Scotland than furth the cottage at Strathan.

Too much advertisement may have a downside if, when you arrive at the bothy, you find there is no room at the inn. Many of these shelters are cramped and few are capable of holding, given consideration, even a smallish group. So, if this were to happen, there is always the alternative of the bivouac. In fact, sleeping out can be advantageous. You can do the lift the evening before and be off at first light. This is particularly true, in my experience, if the comfortable hollow of the night before turns out to be the natural course of the early morning rain. But, even if such ill fortune should strike, you can always console yourself that, given the right time of year, you will have collected a bundle of Munros and be back in the pub by lunchtime.

Nowadays, when mountain equipment has expanded to catwalk proportions, there is access to plenty of lightweight bivvy equipment for those who can afford it (for those who can't, see previous remarks re financial institutions) but when I first started, my state-of-the-art gear comprised several pieces of polythene, a couple of shortened garden canes and various bits of cord. Even my wife, who is of a trusting nature, found the agglomeration a little disconcerting as a necessary concomitant to spending a week away from home. Nor were her fears allayed when I added the indispensable MozKill which, when lit, was redolent of joss sticks.

Another advantage of the early start is that it enables you to catch an afternoon train to your next port of call, where the operation can be repeated. I say 'afternoon train' not to give the impression of a regular service but to indicate that on some Highland lines there is more than one train a day. Most Munroists of my acquaintance regard rail travel as irrelevant to their quest, but they (trains rather than questers) are of more use than is generally imagined. If you take an eight-hour day and apply Naismith's Rule (three miles per hour + half an hour for every thousand feet of ascent) you could ascend 4,000 feet, spend an hour over lunch and still expect to cover fifteen miles on the ground. It is, therefore, reasonable to assume that any summit within a five-mile crowflight of a station is within human reach and that, if within three, it would be the target for an easy enough day.

There are more of these than you might think. The west coast line from Glasgow to Oban allows eight of the greater and thirteen of the lesser.* Where it branches at Tyndrum to Fort William, you can add twelve and six respectively. If you were to base yourself at Crianlarich, for example, all these hills could

---

* In addition, Ben Lomond lies within the suggested circumscription but, as it is separated from the station by a rather large expanse of water, it would require an above-average level of human ability to reach it on foot.

be reached by departing on the first train and returning on the last. Nor is it necessary to stop in one
place. The Travelpass system allows you to shuttle
up and down the system at will and you can plan
your accommodation accordingly. As stations are,
for the most part, within easy reach of habitation,
there is usually no problem in this respect.

Other areas are not so well serviced. There are
only three Munros available on the Mallaig line
but that's the landscape's fault rather than the railway's. If you had been interested in Corbetts, you
could have commuted from Fort William to points
west to your heart's content. The wonderful journey
from Kyle of Lochalsh to Dingle has four Munros
within easy reach and another ten that, admittedly,
are rather pushing the five-mile perimeter but, as the
train is designed to take commuters from the likes of
Plockton to Inverness, there is the possibility of an
early start and a relatively late return. Leaving and
re-alighting the train at Achnashellach, for example,
will give you a good ten-hour day. But this is ideal
bivouac country. Depart Achnasheen late afternoon,
collect Fionn Bheinn and drop down to the Nest.
Spend a couple of days gathering Fannaichs while
ye may before reconnecting with the train at Loch-

luichart. That will make a bit of a hole in the target.

The east coast line is more parsimonious but the stations of Aviemore, Newtonmore, Dalwhinnie and Blair Atholl give thirteen within a sensible day trip and a variety of choice, with the judicious use of bothies. This is particularly true if you alight at Dalwhinnie and make your way towards the west coast line at either Corrour or Rannoch. Utilising the bothies at Culra and Ben Alder, this puts a dozen or so Munros within easy reach. All on your way home, so to speak. Appendix Two details the various possibilities, with a non-corvine assessment of distances together with possible combinations of

Ben Alder Cottage

stations and peaks. Of course, all this is not as convenient as driving your car to the point where the road surface threatens to rip off your exhaust-pipe but if you value unpolluted open spaces...

It would be wrong, however, to pretend there are no downsides. At certain stations, trains stop by request only and if you haven't informed the guard the best laid plans can easily go awry. Also, the platforms can be shorter than the trains. I discovered this to my cost on a journey from Wick to Culrain. A variety of circumstances meant that we had just arrived in time to scramble aboard the last carriage before the train departed. As we approached our destination, the train appeared to stop on a bridge immediately outside the station. We waited patiently for it to pull into position. It didn't and we waited somewhat less patiently for the next station to arrive. Fortunately, Ardgay was only a few miles down the line, but even a few miles can seem a long way when alternately carrying two rucksacks or a similar number of children.

Such experiences are probably good for the soul and certainly tend to make you pay attention to detail in the future. But the learning curve with me is a lengthy affair. A decade or so later, with a high of dartboard conformation settled over Lochaber, I decided to complete a circuit of Loch Treig, collecting the various butts and bens that Munro had invited to his table. The plan was to start and stop at Corrour station. It was very hot. By the time I had reached the summit of Beinn na Lap, I was thirsty. By the time I had reached the highest point of the desert that was Chno Dearg, I realised that I was not only seriously dehydrated but rapidly falling behind schedule if I was to catch the last train back to base. So I decided to abort and intercept the train at Tulloch.

The drawback was that I would be left kicking my heels for several hours at what is little more than a halt. If I had brought any money, I could have tried to thumb my way to Roybridge, with its all-day opening compensations. But I had brought no money or, for that matter, anything much else. The original plan was to travel as light and as quickly as possible and allowed for no more indulgence than an orgy of self-congratulatory ticking. Disconsolately, I wandered along, looking for non-existent raspberries. Then I saw it – a collection of bits of scuffed coloured paper that on closer inspection turned out to be a number of Scottish banknotes. Speed increased, first vehicle thumbed (inevitably, a campervan) stopped and within minutes I was ensconced in the Roy Bridge Hotel.

But there is no such thing as a free lunch. On my journey back to Ardlui, either out of a sense of guilt or misplaced self-congratulation, I could not resist telling the tale to my fellow passenger. As a consequence, I was subjected to a lengthy lecture on how the English – for my fellow traveller was a member, if not an officer, of an austere local mountaineering association – how the English had no concept as to how the weather in Scotland can change in a twinkling of an eye. All of which solemn warning being but a precedent to a lengthy account of how he had found himself in the Cairngorm on just such a day as this, when only the presence of the necessary tools in his daysack, and his prescience in carrying such, had enabled him to construct a snow cave which saved his (and his companions') lives. At the same time he ran the rule over my precautions against a sudden shift from the Arctic in a manner that would make a Regimental Sergeant Major's parade inspection appear cursory. I fumbled off the train at Ardlui, mumbling about a fourfold reparation to the local Mountain Rescue Service.

Killin station

All these minor jousts with fate were put into perspective when I decided to construct and follow a
coast to coast walk across Scotland. On earlier occasions, I had been persuaded by John to accompany
him on a variety of assaults on Pennine peat-bogs
or the less interesting parts of the Yorkshire perimeter. My riposte was to suggest a cross-Britain route
that followed the old drove roads from Dingwall to
Gairloch, with suitable excursions into the surrounding hills. As it turned out, we ascended only three
that were to count. Bad weather, mad dogs and a

tendency for the ancient thoroughfares to turn into tarmacadam surfaces limited our ambition.

All went well, however, until after breakfast on the last morning. We had paid the bill and were waiting outside the hotel for a bus to arrive to take us to Ullapool and then, via the vagaries of the local and national transport system, home – or, in my companion's case, London. Here he was due, on the following day, to officiate at an ACAS arbitration. John is a measured man who is not easily fazed. So his enquiry as to whether I (who had arranged the commissariat and travel) was sure that a bus was due, seemed to be uncharacteristically tetchy. I produced the timetable or, more accurately, my handwritten copy of the same which, combined with the deserted street, did not appear to give him the requisite level of assurance. *I think we had better check.* So off we went to the post office across the road. The drama, as far as I can recall, unfolded as follows:

John: *Excuse me. Could you tell me the time of the next bus to Ullapool?*

Postmistress: [with much deliberation and protracted sibilance] *Ah well now. Around here it is not so much what time* [pause] *as what day* [longer pause]. *But as it is Friday and is near enough ten o' clock* [checking both own wristwatch and the official timepiece] *I think, that if we should look out of the door* [all parties so do] *we should, indeed, catch young Billy coming over the brow of the hill* [which, indeed, he does].

At the time I saw it as but another example of life being conducted at a proper pace and with a due sense of proportion as to the nature of things. It was only later that I considered the implications of the affair. The arbitration, at which John's presence was crucial, revolved around a dispute that had arisen between the workers on the Underground and their employers. It would have been somewhat ironic if the whole of London had stuttered to a halt because young Billy had forgotten to set his alarm clock.

Five
Some roundabouts and a possible swing

It is extremely unlikely that anyone has even contemplated tackling the Munros one by one. The nature of the ground makes it easier rather than harder to pick up two or three at a go. When Hamish Brown did his continuous journey, of which more anon, he had, out of eighty-eight days on the hill, only thirty-six which gave him less than three summits, and the whole journey averaged out at 1,500 feet and four miles per Munro or, in Naismith terms, around twelve Munros per twenty-four hours. In fact, it could not have been long before people began to wonder just what was the ultimate Munro day. This tradition of multi-peakbagging had already become firmly entrenched in the English Lake District. It was started by yet another Revd, one J M Elliot, who in 1864 collared all the hills around Wasdale at one sitting, and reached its apparent climax in 1932, when Bob Graham took in forty-two summits within twenty-four hours, covering a distance of seventy-two miles and going up and down 27,000 feet.

People have since covered more distance and height but the fact that Graham's record stood for twenty-eight years suggests that it is the ultimate Lakeland challenge for the fellwalker who is prepared to get a move on.

In 1964 Philip Tranter completed a similar twenty-four hour expedition north of the Border. His round of the Mamores and the ranges connecting Ben Nevis and the Grey Corries covered forty miles and 20,000 feet of ascent and was considerably shorter than Graham's. Nevertheless, it had a rather different quality. On one hand, Graham's plan was to climb as many separate summits as possible within an allotted time. As a result, a diagram of his route resembles less a logical round but more a circuitous walk by a man who, from time to time, has thrown the odd sideways stick to wear out an over-enthusiastic dog. Tranter's route, on the other hand, follows a natural line, the watershed of Glen Nevis, and was felt by many to be the more accomplished mountaineering day, albeit a rather long one.

However, the Graham rationale eventually took over north of the border and the quest began to see how many Munros could be done in a day. The first, and indeed the most obvious, plan was to extend

Tranter's bag. In 1978 Charlie Ramsay added the five Munros that surround Loch Treig and completed the mammoth round in just two minutes under twenty-four hours, a desperate finish necessitating a headlong descent of Ben Nevis in just over half an hour. Although not as long as the Bob Graham Round, it was considerably more arduous (my own experience is that you travel a third as fast again along Lakeland paths as you do on the usual Munro terrain). Its only advantage over its southern counterpart, in terms of pace, is its geographical position. At the height of summer the roamin' in th' gloamin' can be kept to a reasonable minimum.

Whereas in Cumbria there are plenty of adjacent tops to add to Graham's twenty-four hour tally, this was not true of Ramsay's round. Enthusiasts had to

Farthest north

look elsewhere. The most obvious area was Glen Shiel which, if combined with Glen Affric, offers a possibility of some thirty Munros. In 1988 Jon Broxap duly did twenty-eight. Clearly, by this stage, the whole affair had moved beyond Munro-bagging, or even mountaineering in its usual sense. In fact, a former President of the SMC was moved to describe the activity as belonging to the province of the 'insane'. For the better-balanced who wished to gather a record collection (even Wilson of *The Wizard* would have balked at 284 in twenty-four), the only realistic possibility was a continuous journey.

There had been a tradition of long continuous walks started by Munro himself and carried to early extremes by the Revd Ronald Burn, the first man to complete all the Munros and their subsidiary Tops. As, for the most part, he had to commute from the likes of Cambridgeshire, Burn took full advantage of his Scottish holidays between 1914 and 1927, disappearing into the hinterland in search of his still elusive prey. As he was a poor navigator, he often ended up in places that were not on the original schedule, which meant substantial detours or begging shelter with the locals. His diaries, a bundle of ten notebooks, were discovered on a London bookstall and eventually found their way into the archives of Aberdeen University. In 1995 Elizabeth Allan, using the notebooks both for information and illustration, reconstructed his wanderings under the title *Burn on the Hill.* It is an extraordinary tale of an extraordinary man. It was, perhaps, indicative of his ability to make the most of his shortcomings that, although he had passed the necessary driving test, he continued to display L plates for the remainder of his life.

Eventually these meanderings by various individuals began to take some sort of shape. In the 1960s RAF rescue teams, as part of their training, made a number of journeys that criss-crossed the country, keeping to the high ground. These efforts culminated in 1968 with a nineteen-day expedition that collected fifty-eight summits, and was followed in 1971 by Sandy Cousins who made a solo continuous journey from Cape Wrath to Glasgow, taking in forty-seven Munros *en route.* But it was an attempt by Brian and Alan Ripley to combine these elements that really started the ball rolling in its final direction. They decided to complete all the Munros in a single continuous journey. This particular roundabout of Scotland started in August 1967 and was a valiant failure. After 230 Munros, 1,325 miles and 337,850 feet of ascent, they were forced through bad weather and malnutrition to give up. But others read and wondered and amongst this group was Hamish Brown.

His decision to give it a go was dictated, as these things so often are, by unconnected circumstances. His job in outdoor education with Braehead in Fife had ceased when the school closed and his new job as County Adviser on Mountain Activities had him unwillingly tied to a desk. Brown spread a map of Scotland on the floor and the escape route became obvious. He would be the first man to complete all the Munros in one go. Of course, there were considerations – job security, finance, logistics and, most importantly of all, how, seven years later, should he succeed where the Ripley brothers had failed?

Brown, however, had one especial advantage. The Ripleys were English and comparative strangers to the land, whereas he had already completed the Munros on three previous occasions. Not only did he have a prior conception of the lie of the land but he also understood the local difficulties – Highland weather patterns, the midge season and the potential conflict with sporting interests. The Ripleys had failed, at least in part, through ignorance. The choice of August as the month of departure was probably as bad as it could be and they compounded this error by deciding to travel from north to south. Thus, they set off at the height of midge activity, needed to cross the deer forests when stalking was in full flow and, as the journey would take up to four months, be forced to battle the snow and gales of late autumn.

Brown decided on an April start in the south, hoping for a finish sufficiently early to avoid the worst of midge and animal mayhem. Of course, the cruellest month could have been as bad for him as autumn was for the Ripleys, but Brown was more fortunate. In the end, he lost only two days through bad weather and, on this occasion at least, had his fair share of that element which Napoleon regarded as indispensable when it came to choosing his generals. Moreover, Brown's route seems more planned than the Ripleys'. With the latter, you get the sense of their being driven by circumstance rather than strategy. Whereas Brown, with his intimate knowledge of the network of bothies, hostels and convenient campsites that serve the Highland climber, was able to plan a route that properly included rest days and opportunities for the re-provision of vital food-stuffs.

In fact, although they did not realise it at the time, this was probably the hidden enemy that did for the Ripleys. At the end of the trip, Alan was found to be suffering from a severe deficiency of iron, and no doubt a thorough examination would have shown a variety of similar shortages. It is only relatively recently that professional sportsmen have come to see that a proper diet is essential, not only to produce energy but also to hasten the repair of the damage done to the body by prolonged or violent exercise. The simplest way for a player to retard his recovery after, say, a game of rugby is to retire to the bar. This is not to suggest that the Ripley brothers trawled the Highlands in search of the amber nectar, but it is easy when wild camping to choose food that is light to carry and easy to cook. It will get you by for a bit but after a while the lack of a balanced diet will tell.

Brown, profiting from the misfortune of others, was very conscious of this pitfall. Before setting off, he prepared a great number of food parcels which were pre-distributed around the route. Some were left with friends or, on occasion, with complete strangers. Others were buried or similarly hidden. Each contained the necessary map and sufficient provisions to last until the next port of call. The statistics are impressive – forty-two parcels, each double-checked and proofed against possible invasion, 1,000 miles of motoring to deliver same, 2,000 polybags in varying shapes and sizes. If Brown was going to fail it wasn't going to be through lack of forethought.

But there were also more subtle advantages that favoured Brown. The Ripleys, Karabiner MC members, were playing away, whereas Brown, as we have seen, was very much on his home ground. It is no accident that football teams win more games in front of their own supporters. Before familiarity can breed contempt, it first offers comfort and with comfort comes confidence. Reading Brown's account, you get the sense of a man who knew he could do it. There might not have been the partisan crowd to spur him on but his writings suggest an inner strength bolstered by the sustaining ghosts of memories past. There is also the sense that the walk meant different things to the two parties. One feels that, for the Ripleys, as for probably most others, it was a challenge, something to be beaten, tamed, subdued. For Brown, it seems a reaffirmation of what his life has stood for. Not so much a challenge as, ironically, a retreat.

Unlike the Ripleys, who changed their self-imposed rules as they went along, Brown made up his mind as to what constituted a self-propelled continuous journey of the Munros and stood by it. With the exception of the crossings to Mull and Skye, he was determined to complete the journey without any motorised assistance. The Ripleys started with the same design but circumstance dictated the odd bus trip or lift in a car. Once you fail on one detail, you can be psychologically damaged and this memory of previous failure can seep into and, eventually, swamp the grand design. When Brown patted the final cairn, his utterance of 'Thanks be to God' was not some easily mouthed profanity, but an acknowledgement

The Caledonian Canal

of the particular inner strength that he had drawn on in moments of doubt.

Once done, the floodgates opened and inevitably others would want to go further, farther and faster. In 1985/6 Craig Caldwell also completed a continuous round of the Munros, but took in all the Corbetts for good measure, and ten years later Chris Townsend completed the ultimate Munro experience with a continuous round of all the Munros and Tops. In lamp-post kissing terms, the former, which spread its wings north, south, east and west of the Munro enclave, was the equivalent of adding Sauchiehall Street to the Edinburgh expedition. For the latter, which was not so wide-ranging, the inclusion of Rose Street might be a more appropriate analogy, though presumably without the irradiation that, reputedly, was once on offer.

Before long, there was a new kid on the block. Grahams – a tabulation of hills over 2,000 feet – were produced and offered as alternative, or perhaps further, delectation for the hillwalker in Scotland. They had taken over from the, by then, emasculated Donalds, which had previously scurried around the Southern Uplands in an attempt to produce a list at the same height. The Grahams, confident in their number, limited themselves to summits surrounded by a 500ft drop on all sides, whilst the Donalds, to make a respectable tally, were forced to claim virtually any protrusion that reached the magic figure. Despite the latter's patronage by the Munro Tables, where, along with the Corbetts, they were included as 'Lesser Heights', they had to bend the knee. After all, it is difficult to make a mountaineering case for a summit that, to avoid confusion, is described as being 'at the junction of two fences and a dyke'.

As far as I know, no one has succeeded in a continuous journey of the Munros, Corbetts and Grahams, but in these days of Lottery funding it can only be a question of time. There was, however, one continuous round that was at variance with its competitors. At six in the morning of March 13th 1985, Martin Moran dragged himself from the comfort of the bothy at Luibeilt to climb out of Glen Nevis on to the Mamores. His objectives were Binnein Beag, Binnein Mor and Sgurr Eilde Mor. When he reached the latter, he completed a journey that had started just before Christmas with an ascent of Ben Lomond and, with it, the first round of the Munros in winter.

There is a distinct difference between winter climbing and climbing in winter. The former presumes the existence of snow and ice that requires particular skills with ice axe(s) and crampons on routes that are graded, in the same manner as rock climbs, from straightforward to extremely severe. The latter is tackling the summits within a particular calendar time span. As it was extremely unlikely that all the Munros would simultaneously come into condition to allow continuous winter climbing, Moran settled for the second definition and chose to limit his journey to what could properly be described as the winter months – the end of December to, as he hoped, the middle of March.

An indication of the transience of proper Scottish winter conditions can be gauged by Tom Patey's earlier-mentioned account of the first winter traverse of the Cuillin in an article written for the SMC Journal. Its genesis was three years earlier, when Patey received a telephone call from Hamish MacInnes informing him that the Cuillin were in condition and would he like to join him in a proper winter attempt. Patey, a practising doctor, pointed out that there were some 'trifling affairs' he would have to deal with and that he would ring back in an hour. Sixty-five minutes later he rang to confirm his availability, only to be informed that, as he had not rung by the appointed time, MacInnes had assumed he was not available and had asked somebody else instead. Patey, somewhat put out, gathered some friends and set off in pursuit. In the tortoise and hare race that followed, MacInnes ran into a snow drift and severe mechanical breakdown at Glencoe while the Patey party was racing towards the objective. Once on the ridge, however, the leaders discovered that it had been suddenly swept clean by a westerly gale and any traverse would have been no more difficult than in the middle of summer and, as such, pointless. In fact, three years were to pass before suitable conditions prevailed and a successful attempt was completed.

Moran, on the other hand, felt, with some justification, that the weather during his chosen window would be sufficiently challenging to distinguish his round from Brown's. Most people reared on Himalayan epics and frost-bitten extremities assume that cold is the major winter peril but, given modern gear, this is not so. By far the greater hazard is wind. Even at a relatively low altitude it can be a killer, as was shown in the tragic accident in December 1951. A group of five experienced climbers abandoned their attempt to reach Ben Alder Cottage from Corrour station and decided to retreat the three miles *downhill* to the safety of Corrour Lodge. But to do this they had to turn into a gale that was gusting at over a hundred miles an hour. It took the one survivor seven hours to reach safety. The wind did for the rest, battering them to death. Moran recalls a similar experience on the Feshie hills, where he clung on to his ice axe during the gusts and crawled upwards during the occasional lull. It must have also crossed his mind at the time that if affairs got too bad there would be no alternative but to dig in until matters eased, even though this might be days rather than hours.

And there were other difficulties. Shortage of light compounded by snow of porridge-consistency meant that the days of lengthy summer collecting were out of the question. His self-imposed time limit, however, meant he had to claim an average haul of more than three a day. Hard snow can make walking over broken ground as easy as a stroll down the High Street but anyone who believes this is the norm has either been exceptionally lucky or not spent much time in Scotland. To give himself a sporting chance, Moran lay down his own ground rules – all 277 summits within the allotted span, but using motorised transport where necessary. This concession gave him two advantages. It would save hundreds of miles

Sgurr of Eigg

of footslogging or riding a bike in gale force winds and, more importantly, it gave him the flexibility to change short-term plans to accord with the weather forecast. So Moran and his wife traded in their house for a caravanette, burnt whatever boats remained and crossed the overflowing Lomond stream that was to be their personal Rubicon.

By the end of the twentieth century, it seemed that even the most roundabout way of completing the Munros had been successfully attempted and that those who followed were left with little more than time-whittling repetition. There is, however, one self-propelled swing left in the playground which may not have been fully exploited (the one

Hamish Brown ducked when he took the ferry to Mull and Skye) and that is a continuous journey around the island hills of Scotland. Limiting the challenge to Munros, particularly if you no longer regard Skye as an island, would be unexceptional but by including the Corbetts you would add Arran, Rum, Jura and Harris, and by visiting the island Grahams you would not only pick up the Uists but also add twenty-five more summits to the list. Assuming you close your eyes to the Skye bridge by landing at Loch Scavaig, it is possible to concoct a unique mountain cruise comprising a virtual half-century of hills over 2,000 feet.

Of course, there is no need to have 2,000 feet as the cut-off point. In fact, I would argue that any Hebridean sea/hill adventure which did not include Heaval on Barra was not making the most of the opportunity, but such a limit does have certain practical advantages. In particular, there would be no need to visit the Orkneys and Shetlands and, what is more significant, St Kilda and its outliers. Indeed, if you were to lower your sights too much, you might find yourself in some very awkward situations. To have the best of all worlds, you could limit the trip to the Hebrides (the sophist would argue that Orkney and Shetland aren't really Scottish anyway) and drop the height to include all the Marilyns over 1,000 feet. Not only would this save a bit of time on the Cuillin, but also bring a number of other islands like Scarp and Eigg into play. Serious Munroists may well regard such lowly heights as derisory, but they should remember that the summit of The Cairnwell is less than 1,000 feet above the public road that was probably their starting point.

Once the route has been planned, all that remains is deciding the rules – which, of course, to some is the most interesting bit. Where would football be if we could not question the ref's decisions? Clearly, swimming and rowing fall under the umbrella of self-propulsion and the endeavours of Channel swimmers and Atlantic rowers show that it could be done. But the feat of swimming or rowing all the way around the Hebrides would so far outweigh the hill climbing as to make the whole trip rather lopsided. If the Mainland Munroist is allowed the mechanical advantage of a bicycle, it would be churlish to deny the island summiteers a sail, supplemented by a bit of elbow grease when the wind drops.

There is no doubt that sailing or, rather, dropping anchor can offer certain opportunities denied to the wild camper and clearly this should be borne in mind when alternative route strategies are investigated. As my nautical experience is limited to capsizing dinghies on inland reservoirs, I do not feel competent to offer much more in the way of detail here, but I am assured, by those who know, that considered forward planning could play a large part in any success or failure of the expedition, particularly when passing through the Corryvreckan.

Six
For better, for worse

As with any long-term relationship, some bits are better than others. Unalloyed bliss belongs to the province of fairy-tales or romantic comedies that drop the curtain before anything more weighty can descend. As Munro-bagging is (save for those twelve-league-booters of the last chapter) inevitably a long-term affair, most completionists would be liars if they insisted there had not been days when they wondered why they ever bothered. In my case, there have been occasions when the very sheep were seen to shake their heads at the level of human obduracy. But there are good days, at least in retrospect, and some are very good indeed. The difficulty is dividing the sheep from the upwardly mobile goats. It all depends, when putting together your version of Memorable Munros, on circumstance. What on one day might be humdrum may on another be exceptional, and vice versa. So you are left with the conundrum – was it a good mountain or a good day? How do you pick your top or, for that matter, bottom ten?

Are you recalling a boring lump or a lumpen bore?

At the time it is irrelevant, but if you have cause to recollect your thoughts and commit them to the sight of others, might you not through your selective prism of vision merely be encouraging them to embark on a fool's errand? It was just such a dilemma that led Bill Murray to include in *Undiscovered Scotland* a chapter entitled 'The Six Days' Challenge'. The gist is that Murray's climbing companion, MacAlpine, had accused the author of over-egging the pudding and that his memories had become rose-tinted by the time he came to put pen to paper. Murray accepted the challenge and agreed to pick, at random, six of his original diary entries to settle the dispute.

The first tail on the donkey, an ascent of Elephant Gully on a foul and dismal day in October, goes MacAlpine's way. The gully with its 'vegetation enough to feed all the elephants there ever were' is a poor climb and is left with much expedition. As MacAlpine pointed out, they were now 'getting down to hard facts', which left Murray, to use current sporting parlance, playing catch-up. Ground was gained and, with one entry to go, the score was three-two in Murray's favour. However, as MacAlpine had begrudgingly conceded a curate's egg sort of day on Observatory Buttress, the author knew that if his final piece failed to pass muster, the challenger would claim the better part of the draw.

He and Norman Tennent were introducing a novice, Trevor Ransley, to Scottish winter climbing. The route they had chosen was the Central Gully of Ben Lui. To the cynical mind, Murray's final choice of diary entry might owe more to construct than serendipity, for in many ways it is the perfect mountain day. On the way up to the gully proper, Ransley is taught the art of arresting a fall with an axe. They climb the gully, revelling in the delicacy of tricounis biting into delicately cut steps, before being forced by a cornice to veer steeply towards the summit itself. This is embalmed in spindrift and, although they know that clear blue sky must be only a few feet above them, they are for all practical purposes caught in the middle of a blizzard.

The simplest way to avoid the wind and its attendant snowstorm is to descend the north ridge, which Murray investigates. This is heavily iced and more technically difficult than the gully and there is some concern as to how Ransley will cope. With a mixture of relief and pleasure, Murray noted that their previous instruction and encouragement had allowed the novice to proceed with confidence 'in complete control of himself, and working with skill and pace'. Immediately the mood changed. The sunset, invisible to them, began to build its reflection on the opposing slopes. The climb down continued until the angle eased and they were able to descend to the corrie floor in one great glissading swoop before returning to Tyndrum in the enveloping gloom.

The piece has all the ingredients – the increasing difficulty of the chosen route, a struggle against the elements, the need for considered decision before descent, the pleasure of successfully introducing others to the sport and then the feeling of relief as the angle eases. Yet, when the struggle is over, you finish not in some fetid changing room but in an endorphin-fuelled vista of 'the first dark tides of the night, the death that is the salt of the earth and life's brotherly shadow, flowing and rising, hazily and smokily blue along the glens'.

There was a tendency amongst the generation that followed Murray to mock his roseate passages and quasi-religious investment of what is 'nobbut stanes and watter'. Even his contemporary MacAlpine, at the beginning of the chapter in question, accused him: 'You misrepresent your friends – make them out to be better men than they are.' So it is easy to see why a group of less privileged lads, attracted by the delights of the Peak District, lumped the writings of Murray with the middle-class prejudices they encountered amongst the established climbing fraternity.

Not only was his 'voice' an alien one, but the description of difficulty didn't tally with their own experience. His account of the Crack of Doom (Severe) with its 'microscopic incut holds' or the 'practically perpendicular' nature of Agag's Groove (V Diff) must have appeared somewhat overwritten when compared with the routes that were being put up on the gritstone edges. But the post-war addition to the climbing gene-pool meant that it no longer lapped just below the ankles, and the simultaneous arrival of a number of talented climbers inevitably meant the competition would push up standards and previous caution would be thrown to the wind. Yet, when it came to throwing, I have always felt that, at least for the moderate performer, it was an error of judgment to eject Murray with the bathwater.

And as the majority of Munroists will fall into that category, they will probably learn more about mountaineering in Scotland from the volume of that name

than they will through the recorded exploits of the
Creagh Dhu and its competitors. Most hillwalkers
in Scotland, if asked to name their favourite mountain, would not take the existence of Sassenach on
Carn Dearg or a variety of Posts on Creag Meagaidh
into consideration before delivering their verdict.
Rather, the remembered days that tested their powers and stretched their resources. All this leads (at
last) to what the said hillwalkers would regard as
their mountains of choice. My own straw poll would
suggest that any top ten would include An Teallach
and Liathach and, most probably, Ladhar Bheinn.

An Teallach

It is interesting to consider what marks these out. I suppose their separateness is important. There is no doubt that Ben Macdui and Ben Avon are fine, but they tend to get lost in the surroundings. But there must be more to it than that. No hill stands more separate than Schiehallion, but few would compare it with the Torridon giants. Presence must also be important. As Naismith recognised when suggesting his qualification for membership of what was to become the SMC, the aspirant must have climbed mountains rather than hills. He took the point that 3,500 feet was too arbitrary, but probably felt other compensating factors should come into play.

Although none of the previously named favourites reaches his proposed height, they all start from sea level and so make every foot count, and to climb the mountain properly is not a matter of a quick up and down but of time spent on an extensive (both An Teallach and Liathach boast two Munros) and often, in walking terms, quite difficult traverse along a spectacular ridge. And 'spectacular' is just one of the terms plundered from the Thesaurus. In the hands of the literati, the full range comes into play. Views 'of' are *daunting, wondrous, stupendous* and even, on one occasion, *calliphygic*. Views 'from' are *sublime, majestic, all-embracing,* etc. Nor does their position detract, situated as they are on the western seaboard. The combination of land and water offers a further archipelago of epithets.

I had considered listing my own ten best and worst, but any consideration of the former would leave gaping holes and the latter might be so coloured by the influence of the night before as to be worthless. In fact, the reader might find the whole exercise so outrageous that, like the Bishop of Carlisle on reading *Jude the Obscure*, he would hurl the offending matter on to the fire. Instead, I will limit myself to three days: the one that springs most happily out of my memory, the one that least does so and, to begin with (if Munro-collecting had to be a monogamous activity), my 'till death do part' choice of partner.

The consummation of this particular union took place on a cloudless October day and, though I had no reason to suppose it, the 'parting' – as will be seen – might have come earlier than anticipated. The circuit started at the west end of Loch Glascarnoch on the A835. The first objective, Am Faochagach, humps quietly in front of you and requires a negotiation of a variety of waterways before its slopes can be reached. The route offers nothing particularly prepossessing at this stage, but that is no bad thing. I always felt that the best rock climbs were those where the pitches got successively harder, reserving the crux for the final few moves. Although buried so sheepishly amongst the lower grades as never to bother the present-day enthusiast, Oblique Buttress on Glyder Fach is a perfect example of the specie.

Similarly, with walking, if you do the heavy lifting early on, you can, given the right location, spend the rest of the day admiring the views instead of the vegetation a few feet in front of your nose. The remainder of the chosen round, which includes the Munros of Cona' Mheall and Beinn Dearg, lends itself to such a description. The ground from Am Faochagach slopes away to the north west at a pleasant and easy gradient until it reaches the rim of the corrie that surrounds Loch Prille. On my first visit I was jogging when I could and was so taken by the sudden appearance of the loch that I ignored the lie of the land. I accuse the terrain of mendacity but it was more my carelessness than a hidden trap. An earth shelf that had previously been supporting my feet disappeared and the admired corrie loomed not only larger but, at the approaching rate of thirty-three feet per second per second, somewhat nearer. My right hand grasped at a bunch of heather. Happily, it was not the sort that sets off the wee bonnie braes so fortuitously placed for the benefit of MacScenic Highland Tours. This particular root and branch had withstood more serious assaults on its family seat and held firm. I withdrew, unreservedly, all previous imprecations as to the unwelcome tenacity of this particular plant and continued in a more orthodox fashion to the corrie floor.

Paradoxically, the low point between Am Faochagach and the other two Munros is probably the high point of the day. At the corrie lip, you are standing at the point where the Allt Lair starts a series of plunges before reaching Glascarnoch. From the valley it seems a relatively uninterrupted stream, but below your feet it is a staircase of rapids broken by a variety of lochan landings. Behind your back eagles thermal the age-carved bowl. If the heather, or whatever, has to fail, there are much worse places for it to happen.

The rest is easy. A nice, scrambly sort of ridge to the top of Cona' Mheall and then a graceful curve around the rim of Choire Ghranda to Beinn Dearg itself. The summit commands a view. To the south, the Fannichs, before they spill into the fastness of Letterewe Forest. To the north, Seana Braigh and the end of the Highland plateau. To the west, past the castellated ridges of An Teallach, a ferry – ex Loch Broom – balances its way across the Minch to the Outer Isles. The south ridge directs to your starting point. In autumn, as the light fades, the stags, sensing intrusion, bellow close by and you, in turn, stick close to the ground until at last the land levels and you reach the conveyance that will take you home.

The other two selected days exemplify the original point that circumstance as much as topography is responsible for the nature of the memory. Neither day has a route of the necessary shape to demand inclusion in whatever passes for the *Munro Bumper Book of Fun*. In fact, none of the hills on the happier day would come in many people's top ten, and one on the less than happy is held up as a paragon of pulchritude in such an incontrovertible publication as Wilson & Gilbert's *Classic Walks*.

The better day started when the train stopped at Achnashellach station at a little before six o' clock one summer's evening. The day had had a good start. A long-held whim to complete a journey, sans car, from Glasgow to Edinburgh via Inverness was well under way. Early that morning I had left Corpach on the incomparable train journey to Mallaig. From there, a ferry had carried me down the Sound of Sleat to the Kyle of Lochalsh. Of all the Hebridean waterways, this is the most sedate as it is continuously protected from the more vigorous seas by the Isle of Skye. The eastern views into the hills and lochs of Knoydart are spectacular and the journey itself is just the right length to sustain interest throughout. By the time the train drew away from Kyle, the shadows had started to lengthen and, with my back to the engine, I had watched the coastline unravel its way through the various stations to the head of Loch Carron.

Therefore it is not surprising that when I stepped out on to the Field of Willows I felt all was working out well. The plan was to walk up the road to Craig, then meander up the track that leads to Glenuaig Lodge and bivvy somewhere around the 2,000ft mark. From this vantage point I would sweep the five adjacent Munros and, if all went to plan, extend the outing for a further day and pick up the less accessible Bidein a' Choire Sheasgaich and Lurg Mhor, before regaining the train at Attadale. It was a lovely evening, the perfect hollow found, the allowed measure drunk to raise the outer body temperature to a level that reflected the fading sunset.

The grassy hollow turned out to be the hereintofore mentioned watercourse and the now grey light of dawn was equally reflected by the damp that was seeping through the sleeping bag. It was a little after three in the morning. Sgurr nan Ceannaichean had only recently been elevated to Munro status, so it is possible, in my otherwise undistinguished accumulation, that I could claim at the time to have made the earliest ascent of the mountain in its ennobled state before trudging off to inspect Moruisg. Despite the exercise, I was still cold, damp and somewhat

Bidein a' Choire Sheasgaich

miserable. But, determined to put the 'y' back into whimper, I banged off to Maoile Lunndaidh. At this point it began to rain horizontally and it soon became clear that the only totally waterproof covering I had left at my disposal was my skin. Without a glance at the Sgurrs of Chaorachain and Choinnich, I sloped off in the direction of down, no doubt leaving the wraith of the conqueror of the Matterhorn shrugging his shoulders at the feebleness of late twentieth-century man.

But the valley meant Gerry's and Gerry's meant a dry bed and a chance to dehydrate the gear. This private hostel, a knocked-together row of railway cottages, is different. It forms part of an array of stopping places that have their own place in the folklore of British climbing. It is hard to describe Gerry's but *laissez-faire* comes to mind. My first impression was that there were few of the niceties that the Scottish Tourist Board normally parades to attract foreigners, but this did not mean it lacked style. Hamish Brown recalls Christmas meets when Gerry made 'a fine stuffing to go with the duck – plus all the usual trimmings'. Gerry himself also seemed an interesting man. In certain moods he gave the impression of an Old Etonian who had gone native.

But there is not much to do at Achnashellach around mid-morning and, having hung out the sleeping bag in what appeared to be a half-constructed greenhouse, I noticed that in the battle of the elements, the sun, if not exactly winning, had at least come out of its corner. I then remembered that on the other side of the valley lay the hitherto neglected pair of Sgorr Ruadh and Maol Cheandearg, which the map showed to be conveniently serviced by stalkers' paths and a connecting bealach. It was quite a long road walk there and back but at least it would dry out the socks. The going was so good that by the time I had reached the top of the second hill I realised that, if I really pushed on, I could reach Strathcarron station in time to catch the afternoon train. The choice of this destination would not only avoid the road walk back to Achnashellach but would also offer the amenities of the little square box marked on the map as 'Hotel'. I made it with a pint to spare.

I was by now firmly in timetable mode and realised that if I stayed on the train until Achnasheen, where there was also a square box, etc, I would have a little over a couple of hours to spend before catching the last train from Inverness back to Gerry's. I also knew that, although the Field of Storms might not sound as romantic as a similar acreage of willows, the food the hotel would produce would be infinitely more attractive than the dehydrated Irish Stew that lurked in the recesses of my rucksack and awaited my return. Several quails and half a bottle later, I reboarded the train, somewhat to the confusion of the guard, to end a most satisfying day.

I am sure others will scorn this rather limp offering as an advertisement for The Memorable Munro Day, citing, *inter alia,* Cuillin Ridges and Lochaber Traverses, and they would be right. It wasn't a day at all, for the journey from start to finish exceeded the diurnal unit by a good ninety minutes.

The less happily remembered day began at the moment when an autumn night fragmented into the clammy blanket of so-called dawn. The door of our van reverberated to a determined, if not over-vigorous, thumping. Voices muttered as only they can when involved in a conspiracy. *Is this Ribigill Farm?* We didn't know. We had just parked up for the next day. The Un-Munroist owner of the van had declared that if we were going to come this far north, we would definitely take a look at Ben Loyal. I had not only the obvious plan for Ben Hope but a corollary that included vacuuming up Ben Klibreck on the way home.

So a deal had been struck. We would both climb Ben Loyal at first light and, while Ron pottered around on some bits of crag that he had found scattered around OS 9, I would add the most northerly Munro to my list. As we breakfasted, we became aware of increased activity at the farm. The revving of engines, bellowing of beasts and harsh human shouting suggested that some day of judgment had arrived. But, by the time we had laced our boots and stepped into the dim light of an October dawn, whatever was happening had happened.

The track for Ben Loyal leads through the farmyard and on to the open moorland. Beyond the first gate was a herd of cows and at our appearance a cacophony broke out that would have put the wind up a tribe of banshees. Suddenly all was clear. These were the mothers of *Los Desaparecidos*, the Disappeared Ones. I have always poured scorn on the anthropomorphic, regarding it and other forms of Disneyfication as the root of modern misjudgment. Yet, when the most baleful-eyed appeared to request some sort of explanation before reluctantly moving aside, I can't be sure I didn't mutter some Pilate-like utterance to exclude me from the general blame.

Ben Loyal, I am sure, is a very good mountain. Pictures confirm that, when viewed from the west, it is impressive in outline and in particular detail, but both now escape me. The clouds were high enough and the visibility must have allowed outstanding views, sweeping from the cliffs of Hoy in the north to the range of some of the finer Corbetts in the south, but all I recollect is the view to the east. Here, unlike the western escarpment, the land falls gently away for several miles. I was not impressed. We could have been anywhere in the northern Pennines and saved ourselves a thousand-mile journey. Even now, I am not quite sure as to the cause of my ill-temper. It might have been the thought of returning through Sutherland's equivalent of the Plaza de Mayo, or even the beef sandwich that lay in denial amongst the other survival impedimenta in the bottom of my rucksack. But the fact is that, although I generally have a good measure of recall, the memory of that morning is little more than a blur.

We drove round to Loch Hope and, after the obligatory inspection of the broch, went our separate ways, Ron to return to collect me in due course. I set off up the long shoulder leading to Ben Hope's summit cone. Both the passing of time and the lowering of mist meant matters became increasingly gloomy. At the top I wasted a little time looking for the 'battered woodpecker feathers' with which Hamish Brown had crowned the final cairn of his continuous journey. He had found them on Lomond and transported them throughout to provide an interesting puzzle for any northern-based ornithologists.

It was getting definitely gloomy. The climb had taken longer than anticipated and it was sensible to get down as quickly as possible. It was then I made one of those 'it seemed a good idea at the time' decisions. Rather than retrace my steps, I decided the best course of action was to descend directly the western slopes, so that if night overtook me I would be travelling the horizontal distance on tarmac rather than stumbling through heather. Practice did not bear out theory. The western slope turned out to be a series of craggy drops of varying heights. It was easy enough to avoid the difficulties but the going was proportionately slow. I soon realised that I would not reach the road, let alone the rendezvous, by nightfall.

Still, there was always the torch. I switched it on. Rather a feeble flicker. A bit of a shake increased the candlepower but only intermittently. Clearly, or otherwise, the batteries were on their way out. How often had I pontificated to the less aware that batteries should always be kept separate from the torch, and spares always carried? How often had I played the ungracious pastor! But in this case the way would scarcely have merited the description of 'path' and there was certainly not a primrose in sight. I made further ground, using the torch as sparingly as I dared. Eventually it and I flickered to a halt. I had no idea what lay below me, so there seemed little alternative but to sit the night out. I was examining, with somewhat less compunction than previously, the edible contents of my sack when I saw a light bobbing up and down a few hundred feet below me. Directed by the sound of my apologies, Ron soon joined me, armed with a lamp that would have illuminated overflying aircraft.

Come along, you silly bugger. We're wasting good drinking time.

Seven
The pitch of Munro fever

It is usual to credit or blame Munro with or for the current plethora of hillwalkers in Scotland. But he must have been only one among many who charted their way through Britain's northerly mountains. Between them, aneroids and clinometers at the ready, they quickly discovered all the mountains and offshoots over 3,000 feet and noted their findings. However, the Victorians seemed to require an ulterior motive to justify such meanderings, at least if they were to parade them for public consumption, so the language of the botanist, geologist or local historian is never far from the surface and blurs any real motive. It seemed that if there were to be any profit in their writings, it was to enhance their reputations rather than their pockets and their enthusiastic endeavour was directed towards as much the advancement of science as the provision of a playground for overweight southerners.

The scene is amusingly parodied in a short story by G F J Dutton, 'Finishing off a Top'. The Doctor,

Fisherfield Forest

determined to settle for once and for all whether a certain bump amongst bumps is a genuine Top, persuades the Apprentice, whose dislike of Munro-bashing is only equalled by his disapproval of the ruling classes, and the Narrator to join him on a fact-finding mission. Armed with a Dumpy level and Sir Hugh's very own aneroid ('Patient of mine picked it up at a Kirriemuir roup'), the Doctor arranges the two corners of the necessary triangulation before striding off into the middle distance and on to the point which, in hovering so precariously around 3,000 feet, had confused his august predecessors.

The assistants have to do no more than sunbathe and wave a flag at the appropriate moment. All goes well until first the mist, then the rain falls. Surveying is out of the question and the only sensible course is retreat. However, all the gear, including map, compass and waterproofs, is with the Doctor. The woefully exposed are eventually fielded by one of the Doctor's patients (the Doctor has developed a network for just such emergencies) and over the appropriate measures of Strath Grapple they are cajoled, on the grounds that they were almost there, into having another shot the following weekend.

The non-fictional accounts of such investigations first found their way into the SMC journals and, after exploration had been completed, an account of the various hills was compiled in the District Guides. These were very general in nature, leaving the readers plenty of scope to choose their own way and plan their own routes. There was a sense at the time that too much detail undermined the point of the exercise and that each person, like the pioneers, should approach the hill as if it were a first ascent. Even the existence of the maps produced by the Ordnance Survey did not entirely give a lie to this myth. The Munros, for the most part, were marked, but not always in the right place and, particularly in the far north, the contours on the map did not always correspond to the shape of the land. In fact, some of the marked features, such as cliffs and the like, appeared to owe more to guesswork than close examination on the ground.

There were books, starting with Ashley Abraham's *Rock Climbing in Skye*, that attempted to instruct the reader as to the best way to tackle the Scottish hills, but they tended to concentrate most on the areas where configuration of rock and vegetation offered a variety of problems to the climber rather than proffering the walker any assistance in finding the best or easiest way to the top. Indeed, writers like Murray, although ostensibly revealing the secrets of 'undiscovered Scotland', only partially drew back the veil before allowing the clouds of mystery to return. All this was in sharp contrast to many of the books written about the hills south of the border. These often contained detailed accounts of the paths to the summits, accompanied by maps and illustrative drawings. By the time Alfred Wainwright laid down his pen in 1965 at the conclusion of his *Pictorial Guides*, every route up every hill in the English Lake District had been laid bare and the rest of the country below Hadrian's Wall soon followed suit. But for similar information on the Highlands, particularly beyond the Great Glen, the hillwalker looked in vain.

Then two events occurred that seemed to change matters. The first was the decision by the OS to resurvey and produce a metric walkers' map on a scale of 1:50,000. This replaced the old one-inch maps that for so long had been the staple for the hillgoer. Not only was the new map much more accurate, with the consequent Munro promotions and demotions, but the slightly larger scale made it also more user-friendly. There was more detail, more clearly marked, yet the whole effect was still within a familiar visual framework. Thus armed, exploration became easier. Nevertheless, this improvement could, ironically, have meant the premature death of Munro's Tables and all their attendant interest. There is no whole number that is the metric equivalent of 3,000 feet and consideration was given to changing the 'Munro' cut-off point to 1,000 metres.

But this alternative had little chance of success. The suggestion, if it had been adopted, would not only have cut the list and the challenge by half, but also resurrected the original arguments that railed against Naismith's proposal of 3,500 feet as the baseline for a proper mountain. It was extremely unlikely that British climbers would accept that not only should the Cuillin Munros be regarded as now belonging to the lesser heights, but that also such gems as Aonach Eagach, Beinn Alligin and Ben Sgritheall would be similarly demoted. Those in favour of change no doubt argued the absurdity of 914.40182m as the defining moment. But it was probably that very absurdity that saved it. Decimalisation had been regarded as a bit of a con. Not everyone went as far as the hotel in Bethesda, which for decades continued notionally to deal in old money (the retention of the sixpence as 2½p was for a long time the saving grace), but there are still people of my generation who, when wishing to vent their indignation at contemporary behaviour, expostulate, *Ten bob for a packet of crisps! I remember the time that if you had ten bob in your pocket on a Friday night*, etc, etc. It is at times when we feel that we are being manipulated by foreign interests that the British most decide to become bloody-minded. So, whatever the metric map might say, to some the height of Scafell Pike remains at the easily remembered 3,210.

But what the debate did was to bring this rather arcane activity to the notice of the general public. The fact that a new mountain had been discovered, – or so was the elevation of Sgurr nan Ceannaichean reported – was naturally of interest and Sir Hugh

Aanoch Eagach

and his Tables were presented to the nation with its breakfast toast and tea. This was also the time when the Sunday papers were expanding and specialist magazines began to fill the newsagents' shelves. Travel sections became the norm and their contributors were on the look-out for new places to visit. The mid-seventies also produced two consecutive sunny summers, so the pundits began to feel more confident about embroidering the charms of Wester Ross. More people travelled to Scotland, and in this seasonal diaspora there must have been a number of English fellwalkers who became sufficiently confident to dispense with the Wainwrightian apron-strings.

The second sea change was the eventual publication in 1978 of Hamish Brown's account of his continuous Munro journey. The book, *Hamish's Mountain Walk*, and (probably more particularly) the paperback version of 1980 made life much easier for the aspirant Munroist, especially those who had little or no understanding of the Highlands as a region. Brown's book not only detailed all the Munros in a meaningful order but also suggested starting points, a sensible way up and various connecting corridors. Within one volume, there was all you really needed to know, with clear diagrammatic maps to boot.

The book may also have acted as a stimulant to some. In the Introduction and opening chapter there is the feeling of a man about to engage in some great undertaking, and it reawoke, at least for me, the myths of childhood, those great quests and perilous journeys that led to a variety of holy grails. Even if the pursuit of this particular sheep in wolf's clothing did not measure up to the dangers faced by Jason & Co, it had the shape of an epic. There was even a sense of the essential concomitant risk of heroic struggle which Brown manages to insinuate within his tale. No one had succeeded in this particular odyssey before. The journey would take at least four months and Brown had no way of knowing whether fate might intervene or others might steal a march on his plan to become the first continuous completionist, causing him either to fail or finish, at best, a belated second.

Even if his own enthusiasm is not infectious to all, the book offers more than a route map. Each part of the journey is accompanied by Brown's memories and observations of the places he visits. This was to be his fourth complete round, so he had known all the hills in a variety of condition and circumstance and his recollections give an individuality to what otherwise might be something of a sameness. Armed with these recollections and Brown's exceptional knowledge of his beloved land, there was an incentive to follow in his footsteps and, albeit not in one go, also to complete the same journey.

This is speculation but there must be some reason to explain the increase of completionists. In the decade between Brown finishing his first and fourth rounds, the average number per annum who had ticked the list was five. A quarter of a century later, it was around 200. There are, of course, many other reasons for the explosion – greater ease of travel from the south, more free time and, more importantly, more flexible free time being the most obvious. It makes a considerable difference if you can tack an odd day or two on to a Bank Holiday weekend and thus make the more inaccessible regions a feasible proposition. No longer was it only clergymen, schoolmasters and their like who had the windows of opportunity. Nevertheless, I still have a feeling that *Hamish's Mountain Walk* had a good deal to do with the level of current interest.

Whether or not it stirred the embers, it certainly seemed to breach the firewall. Any scruples that the Victorians might have held concerning the invasion of the sanctity of Nature had long gone. A whole industry emerged. The printing presses rolled. Books were written. Wallcharts (with complete checklist/ progress monitor) and diaries were produced. The concept of what Docharty called 'the creed of the long traverse' found its enshrinement in the imperishable prose of those that followed. Craig Caldwell produced a similar account to Brown's, which included the Corbetts as well as the Munros, and in 1986 Martin Moran published *The Munros in Winter*, his account of the continuous assault on the 277 summits in eighty-three winter days. Further long walks were completed and offered to the altar. There then followed the subsets: *Most Memorable, Least Forgettable, First Fifty – a view from the papoose, Last Hundred – with or without a variety of accessories.*

Even the SMC was forced to reconsider its policy of deliberate underdocumentation and produced a *Hillwalkers' Guide to the Munros*, which detailed the best approach to the various summits and offered other helpful advice. This was followed in 1990 by a similar volume on the Corbetts. The philosophy is laid down in the Introduction to the latter, that is, to be 'a concise and practical guide [... which ...] describes a natural day's expedition [...] starting and finishing on public roads'. This is a far cry from the views of those pioneers who felt that all divots should be replaced so that their successors could feel that they, too, were the first to venture on this uncharted territory. Perhaps, like Winthrop Young before them, the powers that be felt that, despite 'the dangers of detailed guide books', the alternative of leaving it to those who would produce 'climbing information [that was] superficial, sometimes inaccurate, and written or reported from the standpoint of climbers of varying efficiency' left them with little choice.

All this raises the question of ownership. There is no doubt that Winthrop Young felt that the Climbers' Club owned in some way the rock climbs on Lliwedd, if not the whole of Snowdonia. At least, to the extent that it should produce the definitive version of what was what. The SMC probably felt similarly about the Scottish mountains in general and the Munros in particular. In past times, when promulgation was less easy, most climbers would be quite happy for one organisation to gather information and regularly publish its results, but now every man and his mouse can have a website and compile detailed information for anyone to view. What is more, if sufficient interest is shown, the advent of desktop publishing means that it is reasonably easy to produce this information in permanent form.

An interesting example of this was the arrival of *The Grahams – A Guide to Scotland's 2,000ft Peaks*. This was the end result of the efforts of two compilers who had simultaneously produced a set of Tables of their own. Fiona Graham had published in *The Great Outdoors*, a Corbett-inspired list of all hills north of the Highland Line that lay between 2,000 ft and 2,500 ft and Alan Dawson had produced a book, *The Relative Hills of Britain*, that listed every hill with a 150m drop on all sides. By definition, Graham's list was a subset of Dawson's, so the two collaborated to produce a list of 222 (now 224) hills to form the next mountainous tier that lies below the Corbetts and Munros in the Scottish cake. This was, in due course, published by TACit Press as the first of a proposed series of Tables which would include the New Donalds (previously the preserve of the SMC), Murdos (Scottish three-thousanders with a 30m drop) and the English and Welsh hills.

Like the OS revision and Brown's account, these should also arouse interest – if not in the potential controversy, then at least with its to-suit-all-tastes range of collectable tops. There will be a variety of Tables for the ambitious to complete, ranging from the daunting 1,550+ of Dawson's list to the more manageable local conglomerations. But does this increased potential interest mean that the mountains are going to be overrun? If the rate of 200 Munro completionists a year is to be sustained over the next decade, it suggests that currently at least 2,000 walkers have completion seriously in mind, as opposed to the fifty or so of a quarter of a century earlier. If this geometric rate of increase were to be sustained year by year, then by the time the centenary of the first revised edition of the Munro Tables is celebrated in 2021, the Keeper's List could well approach six figures. Clearly this has implications. Not only for the possible damage to the already fragile eco-systems of lino flooring in the various Highland taprooms, but also for the future of hillwalking itself.

Sgurr an Coireachan

In fact, matters might take yet a further turn. Any possibility of a mass market means mass marketeers. Rock climbing is already a primary vehicle for advertising in the US. Men and particularly women, in a minimum of tight-clad clothing, dangle over space in the interests of selling everything from SUVs to lip-gloss. Similar ways of exploiting the hillwalker might be more difficult to devise – bobble hats and peatbogs do not have quite the same appeal – but I'm sure the movers and shakers will think of something and, if that follows the norm, it will look to link Munro-bagging with prime-time TV.

Current practice would suggest a Celebrity Programme that melds the salient features of *Big Brother* and *Round The World Single-Handed Sailing*. On a weekly basis a Group of Celebrities, chosen by the entertainment branch of YouGuv, would attempt to collect as many Munros as possible in a given time. The Celebrity with the least number of points at the end of the week would be eliminated, with the appropriate public humiliation, and the game would continue until the Final Survivor could be proclaimed to the Nation. The show could be entitled *Sudden Death* and officially adjudicated by the SMC, which would, on the day, value each Munro according to the amount of vertical ascent, technical difficulty and prevailing weather conditions.

When the *Climb Every Mountain* concept has been firmly established, the National Lottery element could be introduced. Once a week, the general public would be invited to enter a series of Mini Munro Marathons, the winners and runners-up of each to receive a substantial cash prize. It would appeal to all ages, and competitors would be encouraged to enter into the spirit of the event, with additional bonus cash roll-overs for best fancy dress, most unusual travelling companion, etc. Before long, groups would be formed to compete for monthly and seasonal prizes. Bonus points would be awarded for every set of ten different Munros accomplished, regardless of value. In addition, there could be a winter league, with all the necessary regrading to reflect the noble traditions enshrined in the great mixed routes of all our Scottish yesterdays.

Of course, the media, true to its function, would seize on the inevitable moments of controversy – hitching lifts with quad-riding shepherds, the inappropriate use of feral mountain ponies, traces in the system of Mummery's Blood (perhaps a footnote for younger readers here?) But, despite all this, Munro-bagging will be seen as a sport that is of, for and by the people. As everyone has a view on education and its attendant discipline, so have we all, from time immemorial, walked. We can speak from experience, formulate strategies and tactical short-cuts, write letters to the *Telegraph*. Inexorably from these acorns teams will grow, first in hamlets, then in towns (unfriendly) and cities (hostile). Gurus will be employed to guide their protégés and ply them in their moments of doubt with suitable items of crockery, or whatever happens to be the current *cri de coeur*.

Such could be the popularity that football, and perhaps even golf, will be forced to bend the knee. American entrepreneurs will buy the likes of Manchester United and channel their vast resources into an alternative Theatre of Dreams. The exploding band of supporters will demand parochial success and better facilities. (EC employment legislation will ensure a steady flow of French, Italian and German stars, who will bring with them the necessary levening of *élan*, *intuito* and *Lebhaftigkeit*.) The Swiss will, no doubt, be miffed at their exclusion but will have to accept that they can't have it both ways. Nevertheless, in an attempt to defuse a diplomatic crisis, a Summit of European Ministers for Sport and Culture might agree to all participants being encouraged to yodel at each climactic Munro Moment.

Crowds will grow as the people's game gains ground. Diehard supporters will still cling to their right to balance on precarious ledges, but those clubs with an eye to the future will be erecting executive chair lifts at recently recognised strategic points on the hills. The defining moment will arrive when Randi MacFurless, whose centrefold in *Bolt!* thrutching an E12 off-width in Upper Entwistle Bottom Quarry has been likened in some quarters to Michaelangelo's David, decides to switch codes. 'Rock climbing has had its day', opines Randi in an exclusive interview with *The Clinger and Scrambler.* 'If you want the real thing, then show me some seriously vertical, moss-covered scree.'

More astute commercial concerns evoke the Bosman/Kolpak rulings to allow the introduction of Nepalese Sherpas and fleetfooted Ethiopians. North Sea Oil is drained to the dregs in an attempt to keep outside, ex-Soviet entrepreneurs at bay. Thousands throng National Trust Car Parks to mourn the loss of MacFurless, who plunged to his death while attempting a freefall abseil from the summit of Ben Macdui into the Lairig Ghru. The Prime Minister, acting on information received, awards a posthumous CBE and pronounces Randi the People's Potholer. (*The Guardian*, alert as ever, corrects his *faux pas* to 'poltergeist'.) Much debate follows. There are those who say the great game has lost its way. Retired Colonels of the better class of regiment fulminate and point to the moment when the time-honoured tactic of boulder-trundling was outlawed. Ornithologists report ravens turning pink on a surfeit of prawn sandwiches. Disgruntled supporters publicly incinerate their OS maps. The Queen addresses the Nation on the end of Civilisation as She knew it.

Probably nothing at all like this will happen, so you can come out from behind the sofa. There is a perfectly good argument that the present level of interest is a fad. That people will move on and, like train-spotting, leave only the fluorescent anoraks to carry the torch. Even if the Munro-aspiring number were to reach six figures, the effect could be negligible. The Duke of Buccleuch, for example, could spare every wanna-be an acre apiece without disturbing the view from his bedroom windows. It is also quite possible that there might never have been a real increase in participant-baggers at all. The overall number could well have remained static but, like a plague of locusts, moved from one localised objective to another before eventually departing these shores for ever and descending on the lower European ranges that have beaches attached.

Eight
Life after

The time may well come when you set off for your last untrodden Scottish peak over 3,000 feet. Statistically, at least, it is likely to be Ben More on Mull. The probable reason for choosing the Big Hill on a Headland (though surely its decapitation by the Sound of Mull must have been obvious to even the most careless of cartographers) is likely to be the same as mine. It is a hill that is easily left alone, as a visit has to a greater or lesser extent to be pre-planned. It is possible that you could be idling around Oban when you suddenly decide to jump on a ferry, walk ten or so miles cross country and climb the necessary 3,169 feet before jogging back to catch the last boat home. Possible – but not likely.

Ben More is also well placed for the family celebratory/apology party which usually accompanies the final steps of the completionist. For the possible pitfalls of such an event, I would refer the reader to a further Dutton story, entitled 'An Occasion', where the Doctor inveigled his companions, as a question of honour, to accompany an old college acquaintance on his final Munro. The Reverend Zoar McKinley McSigh MA, BD (aka Old Zero) had ministered to his Wee Free flock with unrelenting diligence and, as such, deserved to be supported in his only fleshly indulgence. Old Zero, of course, was a staunch teetotaller and the outcome when a confusion arose over the Doctor's sixteen-year prized malt, Lochaber No More, and Sister McVittie's Medicinal Wine is not entirely surprising .

Dave Hewitt is currently uncovering the stories and connections of the first hundred Munroists and confirms that his researches so far indicate Ben More to be the firm favourite as the final resting place. In this list of listed there will be a variety of Ultima Thule, but I would be surprised if he has many ticks against Beinn Mhanach. What surprises me even more is that it appears in my own limited edition of Munros measured more than once. On the first occasion, we had put up at the Bridge of Orchy to polish off the adjacent portion of Section 2 of the Tables. We had collected the more accessible summits above the station, leaving only Beinn Mhanach out on a limb. As it turned out, I did it alone. At that moment in time John's Munro ambition was in an early stage of gestation and he decided that, given the weather, an affliction of paperwork was preferable to a soaking. He was not a bad judge. The ford at Auch was no longer fordable. So, inspired by the engineering feats of General Wade and his successors, I felt the drier prospect was to use the high-level construction kindly provided by ScotRail to cross the raging Allt Choillean, before rejoining the approach path at a point above high-water mark.

Secure in the knowledge of the passenger timetable from Glasgow to Fort William, I embarked on a rather airy and somewhat slippery military two-step across the girders. Unfortunately, my knowledge did not extend to the movement of goods traffic, though I developed a clearer understanding of these arrangements as I reached the halfway point on the bridge. To me, at least, life seems to be full of these Macbeth moments when retreat or advance appear similarly inconvenient. On this occasion, I decided to stand still. For those interested in such matters, I can confirm that there is sufficient space between the grab-rail and a swaying goods wagon to accommodate a fairly ample girth. I can also report that Beinn Mhanach is not a particularly exciting hill, which in the circumstances was quite a relief, and upon my return I found that the waters, not to mention my courage, had sufficiently subsided to encourage a knee-deep crossing.

A decade or so later, John must have realised that Beinn Mhanach was one of those isolates which befall the careless Munroist. But, ever willing to make a virtue out of necessity, he realised that this might make an excellent final Munro. Mountain and man rolled out the red carpet to a variety of has-been, wanna-be and what-on-earth-am-I-letting-myself-in-for Munroists, who enjoyed a day, if not in the sun, at least with dry feet. It was not a bad choice for such a mixed party. There is less than 2,000 feet of up and not overmuch chance of too many going astray. Nevertheless, the day was underlined with a little tension. Between the necessarily early booking of the accommodation in which to entertain his band of friends and relations and the due date set for the ultimate ascent, the great and the good of the SMC had decided that they had been underplaying their hand and announced the imminent arrival of eight newcomers. These were not only to be added to the Tables but, more significantly, to John's list of summits yet to be done.

So, the teasing question was whether Beinn Mha-

nach was his final Munro or not. Did the pronounce-
ment mean that the new summits *de facto* existed,
or did they, like Schrödinger's Cat, only have reality when they were observed in official print? Mind
you, it could have been worse. He might have chosen
Sgor an Iubhair, which was in the process of being
demoted from a Munro to a Top. Matters are never
as simple as they seem and this should be borne in
mind when, while plodding up yet another compul-
sory incline, you play the What's My Last Munro?
game in your head. The In Pinn would be a bold
gesture and it would also save expense when enter-
taining the summit party.

Whatever your choice, there will certainly be
moments as you make your last circuit of the track
when you start to wonder what you might do next.
The traditional route is to mop up the hills over 3,000
feet furth of Scotland. When this plan was conceived,
it was limited to all such high tops in the then British Isles, rather than an extended stravaig to include
the Alps and points east. But UK boundaries have
changed and now the highest 'British' mountain in
Ireland is Slieve Donard at a mere 2,796 feet. This
would seem to limit the mountains 'furth' to four in
the Lake District and fourteen in Snowdonia. The

Brandon Mountain

chances are that most modern-day Munroists will have done many of these already, which somewhat limits the challenge. In fact, the determined can canter over each group in well under twenty-four hours apiece.

To make it worthwhile, political boundaries have to be reversed and the whole of Ireland included. This will give a further twelve hills over 3,000 feet which are sufficiently separated to make several expeditions necessary. Curiously enough, the next mountain on this particular list is Slieve Donard, which means there is 200 feet of clear water between the Irish 'munroes' and the first of the lesser heights.

(Paddy Dillon, in his guide book to the Irish mountains, notes this oddity and suggests the existence of such an unusual gap in the list indicates the hand of mythological forces. Perhaps Cuchullain and his cronies were determined to thwart future metri[fi]cation, or any other mainland machination?) Nor should you limit yourself to the three-thousanders. The exploration of the Irish hills, at least if you are winding down, is the perfect post-Munro extravaganza. There is still the big hill experience associated with Scotland, but the access is generally more amenable and the hospitality more readily available.

An ideal plan would be to start in the south west, then over the years work your way from Kerry to Donegal. Passing from Macgillycuddy's Reeks to Errigal in the north, you can base yourself in any number of idyllic spots and explore the hills that cluster along the coast. As with all west coast hills in Britain, they are superior to their inland kith and kin, none more so than the Twelve Bens of Connemara. There is, in addition, much more of a sense of human presence than you feel in Scotland. There are strong religious links, as can be seen by the summit furniture on the likes of Brandon Mountain and Croagh Patrick, as well as literary and historical connections. All this is in contrast with the cleared High-land landscape which so often can have a soulless feel to it. This does not mean that Irish hills are no more than an unctuous Lake District. The absence of blow-by-blow guide books and the eccentricities of the Irish map makers still leave sufficient to engage the enquiring mind.

But there are those who prefer the calm to the clatter and, even after the Munros are done and dusted, would prefer to continue to beat a trail up Route 74. If the attraction is lists and the completion thereof, then Corbetts and Grahams lie in wait. But it may be that one list is enough for a lifetime and your purpose will be better served if you become a little more selective. Moreover, if you have restricted yourself to summits over the 3,000ft mark, there are two distinct areas of hill that you have probably missed. Unless your direction of travel was from the north and south west, you would have run out of Munros before you stepped into the territory of Sutherland or Ardgour.

The former is well documented and often prefaced by the end-on view of Suilven, a stately galleon becalmed in a Torridonian sea. Is there life after Mullach an Sodhall? Try Quinag, Foinaven and Ben Mor Coigach for size. The hills of Ardgour are less

The Pillar

dramatic, though hardly Dirty British Coasters. In fact, Garbh Bheinn is one of the finest mountains south of the Great Glen and Beinn Resipol stands in prominent isolation. But the bonus is the Mallaig line. Alighting at Locheilside, Glenfinnan or Lochailort brings a number of Corbetts and Grahams into play, both south and north of the railway, with an easy return to the fleshpots of Fort William. Other areas have similar hills that are arguably as interesting in themselves but, lying amongst greater heights, tend to lose their individuality. I have been to the top of Carn Ban while wandering around the hills of Gleann Beag, but would not recommend it as a solitary objective.

But the real consideration is whether, when you tick the final number, you are climbing up or climbing down. Does retirement beckon and has the scheme that you have saved for your (really) old age begun to tap against the window? Perhaps not. Such is now the speed of things that New-Age completionists will, no doubt, jog as spryly down their final Munro as they strode up their first. For them, the final Munro will not be the beginning of the end but an end to the beginning. So, if no longer interested in lists, whither they? A simple solution is to return to the better Munros by a different route, or the less good Munros by a better route. Ben Nevis is a good example of the latter. There is no doubt that the tourist path to the summit is one of the least attractive ascents in Britain. Snowdon from Llanberis might have run it close were it not for the unique trainspotting opportunities and glimpses of Cloggy. The path from Achintee offers no such relief. The walker is never given even a glimmer of the great cliffscape that forms the north eastern rampart of Britain's highest mountain. Unless, that is, he or she, to get a better view, strays too far on to a cornice overhanging Gardyloo Gully.

The more interesting approach is to cross the

shoulder above the Lochan Meall an t-Suidhe and descend to the Alt a Mhuilinn and the CIC hut. Shortly above the hut, a great ridge stretches more than 2,000 feet to the summit plateau. This is Tower Ridge, first climbed by the Hopkinson brothers of Scafell Cairn fame. It consists of three separated steps which provide the main difficulties, as the rest of the ridge is at a reasonable angle and is little more than airy scrambling. The first step, the Douglas Boulder, if taken direct, is much more difficult than the rest, but can be circumvented east and west by the gullies that separate its apex from the main ridge. The other two steepenings are the Little Tower, which isn't one, and the Great Tower, which is. The ascent of the first on good holds is probably on the borderline between scrambling and climbing proper. The second, from below, looks impressive and, in bad weather, intimidating, but a ledge, the Eastern Traverse, leads through a tunnel formed by a large block and to a wall with good holds that is climbed to the Tower's summit. Thence, a narrow horizontal ridge falls away into Tower Gap before rising to the plateau. If all this looks too difficult – and if you have not had any rock climbing experience it will – the Traverse can be continued to the foot of Tower

Gully, which is easily ascended to the top.

In summer conditions, the SMC guide describes it as 'a straightforward rock scramble perhaps to be classed Difficult'. But 'summer conditions' cannot be guaranteed at any time of the year. The base of the cliff is around the height of the top of Pillar Rock, one of the more elevated cliffs in the Lake District, and you would have to climb four or five more Pillar Rocks by their longer routes before you would get to the top of the Great Tower. Moreover, the cliff faces north east and will inevitably collect the worst of the worse weather. Even in summer you can be faced with winds accelerated through the constrictions of various gaps and gullies, horizontal hail and wet rocks turning to ice. As such, it is certainly no place for the inexperienced or ill-equipped. An indication of the nature of the task is that, although the Hopkinson brothers were the first to climb the ridge, they could not claim the first ascent. On 3rd September 1892, they reached the foot of the Great Tower but, not knowing what difficulties might lie ahead, retreated to base. The next day they located the top of the Ridge and made a complete descent. Eighteen months later, a party led by Norman Collie made the first ascent in winter conditions.

Not that the tourist path is without its dangers. If you are not tripped up by small children carrying wishful buckets and spades, you are likely to be bombarded by various pieces of shale untimely ripped from their natural resting place by boots too big for the wearer. Indeed, there must be a question as to whether the whole edifice might not collapse under the weight of such general expectation. That, at least, must be in somebody's mind. On my last visit, the outsize waymarking cairns (I assume

North Face of the Ben

to assist the partially-sighted) were encased in steel mesh, presumably on the order of the Lochaber Health & Safety Committee, who had visions of them, if left unfettered, tumbling on to the hapless citizenry below. The only other explanation I can think of is fear of theft by marauding bands of extraneous lapidarists.

Whatever else overtakes you on Tower Ridge, it is unlikely to be the jostling mob. On one three-day autumn visit to the area, we reached the tops of Garbh Bheinn by The Great Ridge, Buachaille Etive Mor by Crowberry Ridge and Ben Nevis by Tower Ridge. On each occasion, after leaving the road, we met no one. Even the top of Britain's highest was sufficiently deserted to let us escape on to Carn Mor Dearg unmolested. It wasn't the weather that kept them away. A high had moored up over the Road to the Isles, smoke from chimneys rose equally untroubled before disappearing into the unresistant air, the sky remained an uninterrupted camber hemmed with cottonwool trimmings. All the routes we trod on this long-remembered weekend had been pioneered before the beginning of the last century and now, no longer of interest to the modern rock climber, lie in a no man's land between the walker and the snow-

and-ice men. Nor is this combination of 4,000 feet of straightforward rock climbing an isolated example. A study of the SMC District Guides will reveal a number of long, technically easy rock climbs that, in summer, can offer a more interesting and certainly less tedious method of gaining height before a good day's walk. In winter, of course, it is an entirely different matter.

My association with The Great Ridge of Garbh Bheinn had not always been so unruffled. Thirty years earlier, I had joined a party at Strontian on what purported to be a sailing and mackerel-massacring holiday. The plan was that, whilst the others continued to pursue their Captain Ahab ambitions, Phil and I would explore the mysteries of Ardgour, with particular reference to The Great Ridge, Great Gully and the big slab of rock known, without much subtlety, as the Leac Mhor. The time was late August and when we arrived at the head of the glen that runs up to Coire an Iubhair, we were confronted by a large and apparently permanent notice that announced that stalking was in progress and, before proceeding a step further, to enquire at the lodge.

So we did and were informed by the head ghillie that it was all right to visit that particular corrie but we must keep to the path on the right bank of the Abhainn Coire an Iubhair until we reached the crag and that under no circumstances were we to approach the corries on the farther side of the stream. We dutifully crossed the river and followed the right bank (with some difficulty as there seemed no sign of a path) to reach the chosen cliffs. We had a successful outing until our final descent became a little confused by the mist. It was one of those days when the fag of getting the compass out of the bottom of the rucksack seemed more trouble than wandering around in circles hoping that matters would soon become clearer. Eventually they did and revealed that we were standing a very few yards upwind of a very large herd of deer. This freeze-frame lasted a second or two before the herd streamed off over a bealach and left us alone on the mountainside. As we knew from our previous instruction that all the local deer were corralled on the other side of the valley, we were surprised to see them but assumed they must have strayed from neighbouring ground.

A couple of days later, the mackerel having been driven off by what looked like a shoal of sharks (well, the one we caught by mistake on a spinner certainly looked like one), we returned to look at the harder routes of the South Wall. On arrival, we were met by an obviously much agitated laird who answered our polite request with the information that the whole thing was ruined and we might as well do much as we wanted. Further enquiry revealed that the deer had fled his land and it was all the fault of a bunch of itinerant youth hostellers who had camped under *his* bridge and, despite their denials, had wandered around *his* land scattering *his* deer in every direction, but particularly to the advantage of *his* neighbour. The trouble with these tourists, he snorted, is that they have no knowledge of Highland affairs.

We could have enlightened him and perhaps saved a lifelong feud between neighbouring clans. But we didn't. After all, it wasn't entirely our fault. This happened a very long time ago and, as befitted our callow state, we held the words of our elders and betters in proper esteem. At the front of our climbing guide there were instructions to be observed when following the directions given – 'left and right means as the climber is facing the cliff'; however, in the case of descending gullies and other such watercourses, 'true left and true right is in the direction of the flow of water'. It all became clear as we walked up the 'true' left bank of the Abhainn on what turned out to be a well-preserved stalkers' path and simultaneously reached the conclusion that men who work and play in the mountains do not necessarily have the same code of practice. We also found ourselves in agreement with Himself that a little knowledge is indeed a dangerous thing.

If the prospect of looming cliffs and lairds seems too off-putting, then perhaps you had better settle for climbing down. A solution is to keep your head below the parapet and concentrate on low-level routes. If, in the sere of your climbing life, you wish to keep on nodding terms with your former troops of friends, *Scottish Hill Tracks*, a publication by the Scottish Rights of Way Society, offers a variety of possibilities. The Highlands contain over two hundred such interconnecting tracks, ranging from drove roads to coffin routes and, unlike their English counterparts, most have yet to be resurfaced for the benefit of the 4x4 motorists. Each route is described in sufficient detail to be followed on the map, and trips can be planned from Cape Wrath to Glasgow or, at a variety of points, from one coast to the other. There are gaps that might, in the past, have proved awkward but the new Access legislation should solve most of the problems.

But before you decide entirely on limiting your ambition, it might be worth considering an article published in 1985 in the SMC Journal. It was written by Ivan Waller and entitled 'That Elusive Final Munro'. On his sixty-second birthday, his wife presented him with a copy of the Tables. A study of these 'mysteries' showed that he had one way or another done forty of the main mountains and a similar number of Tops. Ten years later, he found that he had completed half of the then 543 summits and was, as he put it, 'round the bend without a moment to lose'. Two years later, he became Munroist 207 on the Keeper's List and finally, a year later, he completed the Tops.

What might be worth mentioning at this point is that Waller was no mere peat-plodder. His first ascent of Belle Vue Bastion on Tryfan, accompanied by the strains of a portable gramophone from the Terrace below, not only broke new ground but also added fuel to the debate then raging on the propriety of artificial aid when exploring new climbs. He climbed throughout Britain, hurtling from crag to crag in his legendary Alvis. He claimed general ownership of Black Rocks at Cromford and delighted in showing his friends climbs that he had found particularly interesting. So it is no surprise that, after completing the Grand Slam on Brandon Mountain at the age of seventy-five, his idea of resting on his laurels was to indulge in 'a few nostalgic Lake District rock climbs'.

But what he hadn't realised was that Metrication and Machination were afoot. New Tops and even a new Munro appeared. Waller, of course, did them, though it appears that the sports car had, perhaps symbolically, been replaced by a scooter. To preempt any further orographic eruptions that in due course might be beyond his powers, Waller compiled his own separate list of summits. These he named Metros and comprised all tops between 900 and 914.4 metres, including, as he noted, 'the apt but ominous name of Finality Hill'.

John Dow, the fifth completionist, also produced an article for the Journal to mark his completion. He claimed two points of distinction. First that, as previously noted, he was the only man to have completed the round without the aid of a beard and, second, that all summits were reached after the age of forty-five. Although he made much of the first, going to considerable, if somewhat tendentious, lengths to prove his right to be regarded as the first legitimate completionist, he was more dismissive of the second, regarding a complete round after sixty as something to be the more acclaimed. Waller didn't quite manage that but he put down a marker for the future – a repeat round with your grandchildren? Now, that might be a first.

Appendix One
Munro Gaelic

Although at first sight bewildering to the unaccustomed eye, Munro nomenclature is often quite straightforward. The first word, usually, indicates the general nature of the hill:

A *Ben, Beinn, Bheinn* is most often predominant in some way, either standing alone (Ben Hope), or the most imposing in a cluster (Ben Nevis).

Bidean, Bidein, Binnean is similarly imposing. *Binnein* also translates as an anvil (*innean*), which could give a clue as to general shape and nature.

Carn, Cairn is most often found in the east of the Highlands and is the local equivalent of the above but generally more rounded and stony than rocky and dramatic.

Those beginning with 'S' – *Sgor, Sgorr, Sgurr, Spidean, Stob, Stuc, Stuchd* – are nearly always of interest to the climber, increasing in spinosity from the relatively gentle *stob* through the *sgorrs* and *sgurrs* to the pointed end of the pinnacled *stac*.

'M', on the other hand – *Mam, Meall, Mhaim, Mheall, Monadh, Mullach* – usually denotes a plod up a rounded mound to a summit that is rarely distinguished. At least, the only particularity I have noticed about these features is their capacity to irritate the conscientious Munro-bagger when scouring the summit plateau for the right small pile of stones in the mist. *Tom, Tulaichean* is more of the same but, thankfully, smaller.

Finally, there are the ridges of various width, *Aonach, Druim, Lurg*. At some point along them, the ground will peak to a top.

The next point of definition is to distinguish through size, structure and colouring, eg *Ben More* – big hill, *Meall Garbh* – rough hill, *Carn Gorm* – blue hill.

Descriptors
Ban– light coloured
Beag, Beg – small
Breac – speckled
Buidhe – yellow
Brae, Braigh – upland
Chioch, Ciche – breast-shaped
Choinnich – boggy, mossy
Creagach – rocky
Dearg – red
Donich – brown
Dubh – black
Fada – long
Fionn – pale coloured
Garbh/Ghairbh – rough
Geal – white
Ghlas/Glas – grey/green
Gorm – blue
Leith – grey
More/Mor/Mhor – big

Odhar – dun-coloured
Riach – brindled
Ruadh – red(bright)
Sgairneach – stony
Sgiath – wing
Tarsuinn – connecting ridge
Teanga – tongue
Uaine – green

In addition, there could be further identification with adjacent physical features, eg *Stob Coire nan Lochan* – peak of the corrie with the little loch.

Features
Achadh – field
Abhainn – river
Alt – stream
Ard – height
Bealach, Bhealaich – pass
Bhac – peathags
Choire – corrie
Chraig, Creag – rock
Clach – stone
Dorain – small stream/otter
Eagach – notch, rocky gap
Eas – waterfall
Eilean – island
Fiacaill – toothed ridge
Frithe – deer forest
Glomach – chasm

Laggan – small hollow
Lochain – small loch
Linn – pool
Sail – heel
Sgritheall – scree
Steall – waterfall
Tarbet – isthmus
Toll – hollow

Finally, there is naming through association. However, the passing of time and circumstance can mean that the name has outlived its signifier. You may well see goats on your way up *Stob Ghabhar*, but it doesn't mean you are on the wrong hill if you don't.

Animate
Albannaich – Scotsman
Ba – cattle
Bodach – old man
Bhrotain – mastiff
Buachaille – herdsman
Chabhair – hawk
Chailleach – old woman
Chlachair – stonemason
Chlamain – buzzard
Diamh – stag
Dhonuill – Donald
Each – horses
Fhidhleir – fiddler
Fhionnlaidh – Finlay

Ghabhar/Gaibhre – goat
Gheoidh – goose
Iubhair – yew
Laoigh – calf
Mhadaidh – fox
Mhaighdean – maiden
Mhanach – monk
Mhaoraich – shellfish
Sagairt – priest
Sheasgaich – milkless cattle
Tarbh/Tarf – bull
Tarmachan – ptarmigan
Tuirc – boar

Inanimate
Bhuird – table
Binnein – anvil
Chreachain – clamshell
Chuaich – quaich
Ciste – chest
Eididh – web
Eighe – file
Gaoith – wind
Ladhar – hoof
Meagaidh – bogland
Sabhail – barn
Sgine – knife
Teallach – forge
Ulaidh – treasure

Pronunciation

There are only eighteen letters in the Gaelic alphabet but the missing sounds are made by combinations that include the letter 'H'. Generally, a single consonant sounds much the same as in English, with 'C' and 'G' always hard. 'S' followed by 'e' or 'i' becomes 'sh'. You pronounce 'bh' and 'mh' like 'v', 'ch' is guttural as in 'loch', 'dh' and 'gh' before 'e' or 'i' like 'y' as in *y*ew, 'fh' is silent, 'ph' like 'f', 'sh' and 'th' like 'h'.

The vowel differences are: E can be either 'e' as in y*e*t or 'a' as in d*a*y, I is like 'ee' in w*ee*k, U is like 'oo' as in w*oo*l.

An examination of the phonetic spelling of Sgurr a' Bhealich Dheirg – *skoor a vyaleech yerak* – covers quite a lot of the ground.

A footnote

I fear that all the above may rightly be regarded as rather scratchy. I can only plead that it is not an attempt at a pretentious parade of half-wittedness, rather an appeal to the Munroist. Those who delight in the Highlands could at least try to hold back the wheel that seems intent on grinding minority languages into the dust. The current estimate is that 90% of all languages are under threat and 50% will have disappeared by the end of the century. So will the culture, understanding and knowledge that goes with them. A one-size-fits-all has certain short-term advantages but it tends, by its very nature, to blunt the edges of human potential. Any tongue that has a single word *solas* which encapsulates, in a particular proportion, a sense of calm, delight, comfort and consolation is surely worth keeping.

Appendix Two
Munros by rail

All distances given are station and back or, in some cases, from one station to another. They are meant as an approximate guide to allow the individual to plan his or her timetable, rather than any adjunct to the official publication.

Glasgow–Fort William line

Station	Munro(s)
Arrochar	Beinn Narnain/Beinn Ime *(13 miles)*
	Ben Vane *(14 miles)*
Ardlui	Ben Vorlich *(6 miles)*
Crianlarich	Ben More/Stob Binnein *(10 miles)*
	Cruach Ardrain/BeinnTulaichean/ Beinn a' Chroin *(14 miles)*
	An Caisteal/Beinn Chabhair *(14 miles)*
	Meall Glas/Sgiath Chuil *(18 miles)*
Tyndrum	Beinn a' Chleibh/Ben Lui *(12 miles)*
	Ben Oss/Beinn Dubhchraig *(14 miles)*
	Ben Challum/Creag Mhor *(16 miles)*
Bridge of Orchy	Beinn Dorain/Beinn an Dothaidh *(8 miles)*
	Beinn Achaladair/Beinn a' Chreachain *(14 miles)*
	Beinn Mhanach *(19 miles)*

Rannoch	Carn Dearg/Sgor Gaibhre *(16 miles, returning to Corrour)*
Corrour	Ben Alder *(21 miles)*
	Beinn Eibhinn/Aonach Beag *(18 miles)*

Both of the above are long days and it would probably be better to overnight in the bothy at Culra.

Beinn na Lap/Chno Dearg/ Stob Coire Sgriodain *(12 miles, returning to Tulloch)*
Stob Coire Easain/Stob a' Choire Mheadhoin *(15 miles, returning to Tulloch)*
Sgurr Eilde Mor/Binnein Mor/ Binnein Beag *(27 miles)*
Stob Ban *(20 miles)*

Again, the distance of the above two walks could be split by using the bothy at Luibeilt.

Fort William	Ben Nevis/Carn Mor Dearg *(14 miles)*

It would also be possible to travel to Spean Bridge and return by the Grey Corries/The Aonachs/Ben Nevis to Fort William, or travel to Corrour and traverse the Mamores to Fort William. Both are very lengthy excursions, which would give would-be Tranterists a taste of things to come. Nevertheless, seventeen Mountains, not to mention a further twenty odd Tops, in two days is a tempting proposition for the Munroist-in-a-hurry who is prepared to get fit.

Glasgow–Oban line

Station	Munro(s)
Station	*Munro(s)*
Dalmally	Beinn Eunaich/Beinn a' Chochuill *(13 miles)*
Loch Awe	Ben Cruachan/Stob Diamh *(15 miles)*

Fort William–Mallaig line

Station	Munro(s)
Station	*Munro(s)*
Glenfinnan	Sgurr nan Coireachan/ Sgurr Thuilm *(14 miles)*
Locheilside	Gulvain *(16 miles)*

Inverness–Kyle of Lochalsh line

Station	Munro(s)
Station	*Munro(s)*
Garve	Ben Wyvis *(14 miles)*
Lochluichart	An Coileachan/Meall Gorm *(18 miles)*
Achnasheen	Fionn Bheinn *(4 miles)*
Achnashellach	Beinn Liath Mhor/Sgorr Ruadh *(9 miles)*
	Sgurr nan Ceannaichean/Moruisg *(18 miles)*
	Sgurr a' Chaorachain/Sgurr Choinnich *(17 miles)*
Strathcarron	Maol Chean-dearg *(13 miles)*
	Bidein a' Choire Sheasgaich/Lurg Mhor *(20 miles)*

Edinburgh–Inverness line

Station	Munro(s)
Blair Atholl	Carn Liath/Braigh Coire Chruinn-bhalgain/Carn nan Gabhar *(19 miles)*
	Carn a' Chlamain/Beinn Dearg *(23 miles)*
Dalwhinnie	Meall Chuaich *(12 miles)*
	Carn na Caim/A' Bhuidheanach Bheag *(14 miles)*
	Geal Charn/A' Mharconaich *(14 miles)*
Newtonmore	A' Chailleach/Carn Sgulain/Carn Dearg *(19 miles)*

Mountains served by the East Coast line tend to distance themselves rather more than their western counterparts. As a result, there is often a lengthy approach march before the mountain actually arrives. The judicious use of a bicycle (Bothy Bikes at Aviemore – www.bothybikes.co.uk – for example) could offer a key to the Cairngorms and obviate much of this. As an alternative, a number of hotels will give residents a lift to a convenient starting point. In some places there are even buses!

An index of sorts
(really more of a list)

Un-Munros (which crept into the text, probably to prove a point)

The Baggers

Other Luminaries (including debaggers)

The Books

Abraham, A P: *Rock-climbing in Skye* (Longmans, 1908)

Allan, E: *Burn on the Hill* (Bidean Books, 1995)

Brooker, W D (ed): *A Century of Scottish Mountaineering* (Scottish Mountaineering Trust, 1988)

Brown, H M: *Hamish's Mountain Walk* (Gollancz, 1978)

Campbell, R N: *The Munroist's Companion* (Scottish Mountaineering Trust, 1999)

Caldwell, C: *Climb Every Mountain* (Macdonald & Co (Publishers) Ltd, 1990)

Dutton,G J F: *The Ridiculous Mountains* (Diadem Books, 1984)

Humble, B H: *The Cuillin of Skye* (Hale, 1952)

Moran, M: *The Munros in Winter* (David & Charles, 1986)

Murray, W H: *Undiscovered Scotland* (J M Dent & Sons, 1951)

The Guides (in various guises)

Corbetts and Other Scottish Hills, The: Johnstone, S, Brown, H, Bennet, D (eds) (SMT, 1990)

First ScotRail: Routes 4, 6A, 9

Grahams, The: Dempster, A (Mainstream Publishing, 1997)

Mountains of Ireland, The: Dillon, P (Cicerone Press, 1992)

Munro's Tables: Munro, Sir H T (Scottish Mountaineering Club, 1891)

Ordnance Survey: Landranger Nos 9-57 will do for a start

Pictorial Guides to the Lakeland Fells: Wainwright, A (Westmorland Gazette, 1955 et al.)

Relative Hills of Britain, The: Dawson, A (Cicerone Press, 1992)

Scottish Hill Tracks: Moir, D G (The Scottish Rights of Way Society, 1947)

Scrambles in Skye: Parker, J Wilson (Cicerone Press, 1983)

TACit Tables: Hewitt, D (series ed) (TACit Press, 1995)